DARE TO BE A
DIFFERENCE
Maker

Tina,
You are one of
my best friends and
an amazing sister!
I love you!

Lish

DARE TO BE A DIFFERENCE Maker

DIFFERENCE MAKERS WHO DARE TO LIVE WITH PASSION, FOLLOW THEIR PURPOSE AND COMMIT TO HELPING OTHERS!

MICHELLE PRINCE

Dedication

To all the "Difference Makers" in the world who are making
a difference by following your heart.
Thank you for letting your "light" shine!

Introduction

For many years, as I worked in "Corporate America", I would say to myself, *"I just want to make a difference!"* I was selling software and I'm sure I was making some difference for my clients but not in the way I wanted to. I wanted to help, serve, encourage and motivate people. I wanted to make a positive impact on their lives but I didn't know how...how could just one person really make a significant difference? So, I didn't...for a long time. I continued to work in an area that wasn't my passion or calling. I didn't follow my heart and God's promptings to go in the direction of my purpose and dreams. Instead, I just let year after year go by feel unfulfilled, unhappy and spiritually broken.

That is, until one day in 2008 when I had my "aha" moment. It hit me like a ton of bricks that it's *my responsibility* to follow my passions and purpose. No one can do that for me. I took action to write my first book, "Winning In Life Now", began to speak, motivate and mentor others to live their best life and, as they say, "the rest is history."

What I found over this journey is that we all have a desire to make a difference. We all want to live with passion and follow our God-given callings; our purpose. It's through this understanding that I decided to write this book.

"Dare To Be A Difference Maker", is my vision to have a unique collection of narratives, not only from inspired leaders, but also from those I see making a difference and impacting others in their everyday personal and professional life. These stories are about real people who are making a real difference even on a small scale.

My mission in creating the **"Difference Maker Movement"** and in writing the first of a series of "Dare To Be A Difference Maker" books is that you will gain inspiration, wisdom & the courage you need in order to get through life's tough challenges and make a difference for others in the process.

So many people I speak with these days discuss their issues as though they are losing hope. It is my vision for this book to reach the masses and have a powerful effect on people in their everyday lives. It is my prayer that this book, and the volumes to come, will breathe new life into your mind and spirit and that it will inspire you to take action in order to help others.

I've selected an exclusive group of difference-makers who I know can motivate, inspire and be a part of a movement to change people's lives. Everyone can do this; it just takes commitment and honoring of our unique and sacred gifts. It is to those people, I dedicate this book.

From one "Difference Maker" to another,

Michelle

P.S. Do you or anyone you know, have a story about making a difference? We are currently interviewing authors for our next book and would love to have you join us in this amazing journey. To submit an entry, please contact info@winninginlifenow.com for more details. While one powerful story can be fascinating, many can move mountains!

Michelle Prince

Michelle Prince is the Best-Selling Author of the book "Winning in Life Now...How to Break Through to a Happier You!" She has been endorsed by and worked for some of the most influential, successful motivational teachers and authors in the industry, including Zig Ziglar.

Michelle Prince has embraced personal development, goal-setting and the desire to improve her life since the age of 18. Michelle has taken that knowledge to transform not only her own life; but the lives of millions of people who want to break through to a life of greatness.

Aside from being an author, Michelle is a sought after motivational speaker, one-on-one mentor and radio show host on the "Winning In Life Now Radio Show". She owns her own company, Prince Performance Group as well as her own publishing company, Performance Publishing. She has hosted Ziglar's Success 2.0 LIVE webcasts and has been featured on SIRIUS Satellite Radio as well as several syndicated radio shows around the country. She was recently awarded the "2010 Goal Achievement" award by hitting more goals in the last 18 months than 97% of people do in a lifetime.

Michelle's style is one who can see your greatness and help you manifest that into action. She will help you to reach higher and go farther with her support and encouragement along the way.

Contact information for Michelle is 469-443-8768, Info@PrincePerformance.com or www.WinningInLifeNow.com.

Table of Contents

Chapter
1

Overcoming Negative Limiting Beliefs

Finding My Value

by John Boaz

Development of Low Self-worth

I was raised in a mobile home park right next to a nice golf course community. My family consisted of a dad, mom, and younger sister. We were considered a nice family, but labeled "white trash." At twelve years of age I began to realize that we were poor. I started noticing where we lived in comparison to where others resided. I recognized that my friends had "normal" houses and that my mobile home, which had no air conditioning, no heat, holes in floor and roof, was not like the homes of my friends.

I remember my mother sitting me down at that time and asking if I wanted to move to a "normal" house or stay in the mobile home. Of course, a twelve-year-old boy is most likely going to answer that he would like to live in the same type of house as his friends. What I did not know then, but found out a few weeks later, was that my mother used that as a rationalization to leave my dad. She wanted what was best for us, so she took my sister and me to live with relatives in Oklahoma. We got that "normal" house, but it came at a high price.

After a year of living with my mom, I left and moved back to the mobile home park with my dad. During this time I was struggling dealing with the divorce of my parents and was now in the middle of a custody battle between them.

Just six months later, I was at a friend's house and suddenly blood began to drip from my left ear and I could not stop vomiting. We panicked, but managed to find an adult who could drive me to the local doctor. I remember my dad showing up at the hospital and then the doctor gravely stating, "He may not make it."

After two weeks I woke up in the hospital to find that I had suffered a brain aneurysm. The first sounds I heard were my parents fighting over who should be allowed in the room and who should be making the medical decisions. I was bald as the doctor's had shaved my head, and a 12-inch scar with 30 staples created a railway path down the back of my head to my neckline. This surely didn't help my self-image.

Another six months went by and my neurologist requested that an MRI be performed. To this point all I had done was a CAT Scan because at the time MRIs were new and very costly. The test was completed and it revealed that a brain tumor had caused a blood vessel in my head to burst. Surgery was immediately scheduled to remove the tumor the following week.

I woke up a few days after surgery to a gentleman shocking my face with a small electrode. At this point I was close to the end of my patience with all of this surgery stuff, when the doctor and my parents came to the bed and told me, "We have good news: the tumor is completely removed. We also have some bad news." It seemed the tumor had grown around my auditory nerve and my eighth cranial nerve. Even though the tumor had been removed, this meant that I would be permanently deaf in my left ear and I would not be able to move the left side of my face, similar to a patient with Bell's palsy.

The Time of NO Self-Worth

At the young age of fourteen, I came to the difficult understanding that I was poor, my parents didn't love me (or each other), enough to stay together, I was deaf, and I had a deformed face.

I had also been scheduled for another surgery. This one was to harvest a nerve from my tongue and graft it into my neck, in the hope that it would grow into the left side of my face and provide some muscle tone. The surgery was a success as the doctor stated that I would not regain movement on the left side of my face but I would have tone, thus the left side would not droop down.

My Solution to the Problem

Still fourteen, I took an inventory of all the things in my life and decided that I was not as good as the smart, attractive, affluent kids whose parents were still together. I became so self-conscious of how I looked that I felt comfortable only being around the people who I knew would not judge me. I found a new group of friends—a group that probably had the same self-worth issues that I had but for different reasons. This group did drugs, drank beer, stole things, and got into a lot of fights. I could fit in here because they did not care what I looked like; they just cared whether or not I would do the drugs, drink the beer, steal the car stereo, or fight the big guy in the other group.

I also found that I was valuable to this group of people. In my adolescent mind I did not see myself as valuable to my parents, because if I was, in my way of thinking, they would have stayed together. I drank the most, ran the fastest from the cops, stole the most expensive car stereos, and fought the toughest guys. I was cool—this group did not judge me, they loved me.

This pattern carried over into my college years. I found a group that I could be valuable to by being the biggest drunk. They weren't a bad group of kids, they were just immature. Nobody in this fraternity seemed to be too concerned about the well-being of the others. We were all just trying to figure out life on our own.

After college, I needed to work and I found myself employed in a sales position. This is the worst possible position for a guy who cannot smile and thinks that everyone who sees him stares at his deformed face. The position was in healthcare, and I needed to get patient referrals from local healthcare providers to do my job. One way I thought I could build quick credibility in the local healthcare community was to deliver "Meals on Wheels" to the elderly. This seemed to be a surefire way to let people know I really did care and would thus receive referrals for my job.

The Right Step for the Wrong Reason

In 1996, I delivered my first meal. My route was located in Plano, Texas, and I was to take a small tin-box meal into the home of a senior once a day. My first delivery went like this: I knocked on the front door of a home; a little old lady opened it, smiled, and asked me to put the food on the counter, after which she asked me to sit down and talk. I sat on the couch and she told me about her husband and kids, and how long she had been in her house. We ended up talking for about ten minutes, after which she gave me a hug and a kiss on the cheek. She had a smile the size of Texas.

At the next house the same thing happened again. And again. I dropped off ten of these meals and then I went back to work.

After a year of delivering meals, I noticed a significant change in my life. I started to realize that I had a new group of friends outside of the elderly community. Many in this group were well-educated, family-focused people, and were successful in the business community. I had dropped most of the friends from my past and was feeling better about myself.

I did some serious reflection to figure out why I was now associating with a better group of people. It turned out that during that year of delivering for "Meals on Wheels" I had begun to build my self-confidence and I found myself having value to this small group of people. I had become valuable to a group of little old ladies who often had no one else to talk to during their day. I gave them a small portion of my time and they gave me their love through a simple hug and a kiss on the cheek. For the first time in eleven years, I felt I had value.

My Purpose was Hand-delivered

I wondered what it was about this group of people that allowed me to be myself. I realized that they do not judge. They didn't care what I looked like. They didn't care that I couldn't move the left side of my face. They didn't care that I couldn't hear in one ear. They just wanted someone to care that they were still alive!

At that precise moment I found my purpose, my mission, and my passion. I knew that this was what I was supposed to do. This group of older adults provided me with an inner healing that transformed the way I viewed myself and the way I lived my life. I know deep in my heart that I am supposed to care for the elderly population because they cared for me when I thought no one else did.

I am humbled to say that I've achieved amazing business success in a short period of time. In 1997, I opened my first assisted-living home and continued building more facilities over the following five years. In 2003, I opened Reliant Home Health with offices in Dallas and San Antonio, TX, and most recently, in 2011, I opened a 50-bed Alzheimer's assisted-living community called Sundance at Oakhill.

Because of my business success, I've been able to share my experience and financial resources to further the success of other organizations, such as the Collin County Community on Aging, the Foundation for Allen Schools, the Network for Teaching Entrepreneurship, and the Vistage CEO Leadership Group.

I don't say these things to try to impress you, but rather to show that once I focused on helping others, my whole career and life turned around for the better. In the business world, I thought that I could not compete with a guy who had an MBA or PhD. I felt I was not "smart enough" to go head-to-head with "real" businesspeople. What I think I discovered about myself was that I could certainly "out-care" others. With this new path I will always be in a business where I "sell" care, and I will care more than my competition, and the Lord will provide a way for that care to be enough to be successful.

How God Answers Prayers

God does not answer our prayers the way we expect him to. For many years I prayed for my hearing to come back and for the left side of my face to work. Even though neither has happened, God answered my prayer in a way that I truly needed. He pointed out that my direction in life was to care for the elderly and used them to show me how valuable I can be to others, and ultimately, how valuable I am to Him. Rather than healing my deformity to make me look "normal" to the world, he showed me a world that didn't care what I looked like. Amazing! ■

John Boaz

John Boaz is 39 years old and the founder of six companies that serve our aging population. He currently holds the CEO position at three companies and sits on the board of four non-profit organizations. John suffered from a brain aneurysm at the age of 14 and spent the next 12 years lonely, poor, sad, and suffering from extremely low self-esteem. At the age of 25, he started delivering "Meals on Wheels" and found his "value" and "purpose." As a way to give back to his community, he has spent the last 14 years building companies that serve seniors. In 2010, John's companies provided over 27,000 home nursing visits to more than 800 seniors living at home or in retirement communities. He and his wife reside in North Texas with their four children which he will tell you are going to each make a difference in the world by helping others.

For more information contact John at boaz@relianthomehealth.com, 1101 Raintree Circle, Suite 180, Allen, TX 75013 or 972-390-7733.

Make a Decision, Not an Excuse

by John DiLemme

Theodore Roosevelt once said, "In any moment of decision, the best thing you can do is the right thing, the next best thing is the wrong thing, and the worst thing you can do is nothing." In life, we make decisions everyday. Some are so habitual that we don't really even have to make a conscious decision, we just do it. Others require a little more thought, but we usually follow through based on our better judgment. The most important decisions make us consider all factors involved and then we struggle with our final choice. It's like a mental tug-of-war. As President Roosevelt pointed out, the worst thing that you can do at that point of uncertainty is nothing.

When faced with a tough decision, have you ever said, "I'll have to think about it?" I know I have on several occasions. However for many people, the "thinking about it" process drags out and becomes the "I'm avoiding making a decision" phase. It's smart to weigh your options, ask the advice of colleagues, and consider alternatives; however, simply not making a challenging decision is irresponsible. It's not just going to go away. It will still be there when you wake up every morning and will hang over you like a dark cloud until you take action.

What's worse is that the failure to make a decision is progressive or should I say regressive. After the "I'm avoiding making a decision" phase, you start to ease the stress of the decision by making excuses. I've heard every excuse in the book. It's really amazing what someone will say just to avoid making a decision. The worst is when the excuse is a complete lie. Not only has the action moved from an excuse to lying, but remember the words that we speak often come true, so be careful what you say to get out of simply making a decision.

Instead of engaging in all that foolishness and wasting everyone's time, look at the decision as an opportunity. You have been given the power to make a significant change in the world by the choice that you make. Now, I'm not going tell you that that choice will be right 100% of the time, but how will you ever know if you don't step out in faith and take that risk? Every hard decision takes courage.

On September 19, 1999, twenty year old Jaqueline Saburido and four friends were on their way home from a birthday party when an SUV driven by a drunk driver slammed into their car. Within minutes, the car caught fire and Jacqui was pinned in the front seat. She suffered burns over 60% of her body and her chances of surviving were slim. Jacqui lived, but her injuries were devastating.

She lost her hair, ears, nose, and her hands were so badly burned that all of her fingers had to be amputated. Her left eyelid was removed and most of her vision is gone. Jacqui has had more than fifty operations since the crash and has many more to go. It would have been easy for Jacqui to give up at any point, but she made the courageous decision to keep living her life. Jacqui continues to tell her story worldwide and speaks out against drunk driving in national campaigns.

What if she had made the decision to give up? It would have been so easy for Jacqui to lock herself away from the world forever and use every excuse available not to continue her fight. No one would have blamed her if she did. During an interview, Jacqui said, "If you want to do anything, never give up. You need to keep going. Continue to live. Whatever happens in your life, you need to keep going and be happy." Through her courageous decision to keep going, Jacqui has touched the lives of millions worldwide, but more importantly, she has saved the lives of hundreds, possibly thousands, as an advocate against drunk driving.

You have the chance to change lives with your decisions too. At the heart of every dream is the desire to touch the life of another person. I have many students that dream of achieving a certain level of success so that they can help other people. Ultimately, if they fail to make a decision to stay committed to that dream, then those people that they dreamed of helping will remain in the same position. Is that a harsh statement? Yes, but it's absolutely true.

One of my elite coaching clients dreamed of building one hundred orphanages in India. She had even toured the devastated areas and seen the orphan children eating out of garbage cans. Those images stuck with her as she built her business, but she was still full of excuses as to why her business wasn't growing more rapidly. It didn't take long to figure out that she wasn't implementing all of the strategies that she had learned from our coaching, and the result was a business plateau. Basically, her business wasn't declining, but it wasn't growing either.

Once she figured out that SHE was actually causing her dream of building one hundred orphanages to slip away, she stopped all the excuses and made the decision to start building her business the right way. Why? Because she realized what was at risk if she didn't make the right choice. What's at risk for you? Is your failure to make decisions worth the loss of your dream?

At this moment in your dream building process, your life is in your hands. You have the ability to make a decision versus an excuse. You are either stepping out or standing up in decision land, or you are lazily sitting in excuse land. You're either achieving your dreams through making decisions, or you're waving your dreams goodbye as you're making excuses. You have the God-given ability to make a decision versus making an excuse so use it.

One of my favorite quotes is "Decision plus action equals

results." You first have to make the decision and then take the needed action to create the results that you desire. This works both for us and against us. Let me give you an example. If you make the decision that you want to lose weight and you take the action of exercising for an hour a day, then you will likely achieve the result that you desire. However, if you make the decision to lose weight and your only action is sitting on the couch all day watching television, then you will likely achieve undesirable results. Like I said, "Decision plus action equals results." It's inevitable!

Excuses are always followed by reasons of why you can't do something. "I can't build my business because I don't feel like prospecting. I can't read this book because I get a headache reading that much. I can't attend the seminar because I don't have time and it costs too much." When you make an excuse, you instantly plant a seed in your mind that you are incapable of doing something. This is personal self-destruction. Every excuse destroys a little bit of belief in yourself and your ability to achieve your dream.

Without self-belief, there is no motivation to succeed. That's the main reason that I spend so much time immersing myself in personal self-development in the morning before I start my day. Success and motivation is the first thing I hear and see in the morning and the last thing that I allow to go into my spirit as I drift off to sleep. Why am I so disciplined? Because I know that I could never overcome the adversity that I face daily if I didn't continually reinforce my belief in myself and my dreams. More importantly, I would not be confident in the decisions that I make without that belief.

When you start to question your abilities, you further put off making the decision, which is better known as procrastination. Psychologists often cite procrastination as a mechanism for coping with the anxiety associated with starting or completing any task or decision. Now I don't always agree with what the so-called experts say, but this is a point that I agree with 100%. It's like a breath of fresh air when you push the decision aside and stop letting it worry you for a while. However, procrastination is just a temporary fix. It's much more stressful to just let the decision hang over your head and possibly get more difficult as time goes by. Like I said before, simply not making a decision is irresponsible. Procrastination will also make you lazy. Do you really want to be known as lazy and irresponsible?

Understand that you have the right to live your dream, but you have to crawl out from under the pile of excuses that have built up and make a decision to change. Inside the word challenge is change. You have to be willing to change the way you handle challenging decisions. You can't just remain where you are forever. Remember, decision plus action equals results. Take a look at your results. Are you completely satisfied with your success level in every area of your life? Reread that question. I said "completely satisfied." I did not say comfortable or complacent. To be completely satisfied means that you have achieved every level of success that you can possibly achieve in that area of your life. Personally, I don't know anyone like that.

I'm not just talking about the amount of money that you have in the bank. I want you to really think about every area of your life —physical, social, mental, and financial. If you're not happy with your results in those areas, then it's time that you make a decision about where you want to be and what you're willing to do to get there. You need to make a decision and stick with it.

Your decisions must be based upon your *Why*, which is your ultimate purpose in life. It is the foundation for every single decision that you make. Without a *Why*, a focus for your life, your decisions will be aimless and haphazard. Your life will be without direction. When you go on a road trip, you have a plan of action and most importantly directions. You don't say, "I want to get from Miami to Los Angeles in three days. I'll just keep going in a northwest direction. I'm sure I'll get there eventually." You may get there eventually, but you will waste time and resources and likely become frustrated that you simply didn't grab a map.

Do you understand what I'm trying to say? Without your *Why*, you are living without a destination. You are without purpose, without aim, without direction. You will be like a piece of paper that's just blowing along with the wind, just going with the flow. That's fine if you have no goals and want to be a spectator in the game of life. Come on! You and I both know that's not what you want! You want to be remembered for the life that you led and the lives that you changed.

I challenge you right now to expand your *Why*. The stronger and bigger your *Why*, the more decisive you'll become in your daily actions. If your *Why* is weak, you will eventually lose all motivation to achieve success. If you're not emotionally connected to your *Why*, you will abandon your goals and dreams at the first sign of defeat. Remember, your *Why* in life is your foundation for every decision that you make. How can you really expect to make wise decisions if your foundation has cracks in it? You can't! Instead, stand strong on your *Why* in life and truly believe that the ultimate achievement of your *Why* is possible.

Make a commitment to get focused on making new and better decisions by believing in your *Why*, building your self-belief, and stopping all of the excuses. Your daily actions will determine your future, and your actions are halted every time you make excuses to stop moving in the direction that leads you to your *Why*. Just imagine that you get in your car to go to the store. You are traveling at a good rate of speed and then you reach a stop sign. No problem… you stop. As you are about to accelerate, you see another stop sign and then another and then another. It's not long before you are stopping so much that it seems as if you are never going to reach your destination. You become frustrated and just go home. That's what happens when you make excuses too! You are no longer progressing in your daily action steps that will assist you in achieving your next level of success. Excuses take over and you take three steps back with every excuse. Before long, you are back where you started and ready to just give up.

If you haven't figured it out yet, excuses challenge me. Every time that I hear an excuse, I hear fear. Fear is much easier to deal with than an excuse. An excuse can be justified. You can create a whole long list of reasons why your excuse is valid. Let me give you an example. I remember a coaching client that was scheduled to show her business plan to a potential client. We had practiced her plan many times so I knew that she was ready. She had rescheduled the appointment several times and gave me plenty of excuses why—sick child, worked late, no transportation, blah, blah, blah. When she ran out of excuses and reasons to back up those excuses, she was faced with the real reason that she didn't follow through on her decision... FEAR.

She was so afraid that she would fail that she made up excuse after excuse to try to get out of it. I told her to stop the excuses and take charge of her life! She increased her daily affirmations and the amount of time that she invested in personal development. She rebuilt her belief in herself and faced her fear head on. Within a few weeks, she stopped making excuses, showed the plan, and enrolled a new person in her business.

Fear tolerated is faith contaminated. There's simply no way that you can step out in faith to achieve your dream if you continue to allow fear to steal your belief. That's right. I said it! YOU are allowing fear to determine your level of success in life. Many people try to play the old blame game, but the only way that you can defeat fear is to stand up to it.

Think about the story of David and Goliath. You have a giant named Goliath that was believed to be over nine feet tall. Then you have David, who was so small that his body armor kept falling off. David didn't let the size of Goliath intimidate him. Instead, he walked toward the giant and prepared for battle. Goliath laughed and taunted David. Well, we all know that it didn't work out so well in the end for Goliath. If fear is your Goliath, then it's time for you to face it and extinguish it out of your life for good. There's simply no way that you can achieve the next level of success until you conquer fear.

Fear is also your body's natural reaction to stress. The body doesn't like to be stressed. It wants to remain relaxed and doesn't want to be challenged. That's why so many people eventually give up on their dream. They're not willing to challenge their body's attempt to remain in that comfort zone. As a champion, I know that you're willing to become uncomfortable and make decisions that will ultimately change your life for the better. As your coach, I'm here to challenge you and to help you make those decisions that will move you forward towards the achievement of your goals and dreams.

Let's dig a little deeper and see how your decisions are holding you back from living the life that you've always dreamed of living. I want you to write down three most challenging areas of your life. It could be finances, relationships, physical health, etc. What areas in your life are you really unhappy with at this time? Don't go any further in this reading until you've made this list.

The one thing that we just have to get out of the way before we proceed is the realization that it's your fault. That's right. Your decisions have created problematic situations in these three areas of your life. I want you to take responsibility for your decisions that have produced these poor results. Remember, decision plus action creates results—positive or negative. Yes, it's hard to admit that you are failing in some way, because of your own decisions or failure to make decisions. Let's move on to better news.

Remember, I'm here to challenge you, and the following questions won't be easy to answer. We're going to focus on how you can move forward and learn from those decisions instead of just settling for your current life results. We will look at your *Why* and get decisive on building that *Why*. After all, your *Why* in life is your foundation for the decisions that you make so let's make sure that it's strong enough to withstand hurricane force excuses.

The first question that I'm going to ask you is life changing. Do your daily actions violate your *Why*? When I say the word violate, what do I mean? To violate something means to go against something. If you violate a law such as not stealing, you're going to pay the price. Even if you don't suffer the consequences right away, sooner or later, you're going to pay the price for your wrongdoing. A law is put in place to protect you and benefit you. When you go against it, your own protection and benefit is compromised and put at risk.

Are your daily actions violating or empowering your *Why*? Take a look at what you do everyday and really think about the possibility that those daily action steps are compromising your success. The root of change lies in your daily decisions. I just cannot stress enough the vital role your daily decisions play in shaping your life. I'm not concerned right now with your outward success. Your current level of success is based on all of the decisions that you've made up to this point. We're going to rebuild your future decisions. Your future decisions need not have anything to do with your past decisions. Once you choose to go in a new direction, your decisions will automatically change as a result. Instead of looking backwards at your past, you must look forward towards your future.

Now, take a good look at those three areas of your life that you want to improve. I want you to get committed to examining them and taking responsibility for them. Here's the harsh reminder again. Where you are in your life is YOUR responsibility, and no one else's. Your life has been shaped by the decisions that you've made. Not your spouse, not your children, not your friends, and not even your enemies are at fault for the decisions that you've made throughout your life. If you don't take responsibility for the current state of these three areas of your life, you'll never be able to change them.

If you're going to get committed, it is absolutely crucial that you take responsibility for the current state of these three areas right now! If you're not willing to take responsibility for your life, then you might as well stop reading this chapter. Go ahead and put this book down. I say this because until you take full responsibility for your life, you will never move forward and claim the life that you want to live. Have you taken full responsibility for your life? If so, read on.

I want you to examine the three areas of your life that you want to change. Ask yourself right now, "What action steps can I take today that will allow me to reshape my future? What can I do today to help move me from where my life is now to where I want my life to be?" Do you want to achieve your *Why* bad enough to make new decisions? Is your *Why* worth pursuing regardless of the cost? Are you willing to face the criticism that will accompany you in your journey? Remember, when you start to change your life for the better, your enemies pop up. People begin to challenge you. You've got to be prepared for those challenges that people will present you with. If you've already met those enemies and you're still moving forward towards your dreams, you're doing a fantastic job! I am so proud of you for staying committed and for challenging your enemies every step of the way.

When you make a decision to follow your *Why* and do whatever is necessary to reach it, you must have faith. You must have faith in yourself and in the process. When you plant a seed, you don't keep digging it up everyday to see if it's still there. Why not? Because you know that if you continually dig up the seed, then it's not going to grow. You have to plant the seed, put the soil on it, and allow nature's seasons to harvest it. Just like nature goes through seasons, your life goes through seasons too.

There's a reason for every season that you go through in life. It's not always easy to understand at the time that you are going through it, but is often revealed in the future. One principle that is constant through every season is sowing and reaping. It's been proven that whatever you sow in life, you will eventually reap. Sowing and reaping will never cease. If you don't believe it, then just take a look back at the bad decisions that you've made. What were the results of those bad decisions? In other words, what did you reap from those bad decisions? Flip that around. What have you reaped from your good decisions? You plant a bad seed—you get a bad harvest. You plant a good seed—you get a good harvest. It's really just common sense.

I talk a lot about sowing seeds of greatness in the lives of others to reap a bountiful harvest. I'm not talking about just donating money to charity or buying presents for kids at Christmas. Those are great things, but you can also sow seeds with your words and your actions. Speak prosperity into the lives of others. I love to hear parents speaking life into their small children. "You are a champion. You can do all things. I am so proud of you." Those are seeds of greatness that those parents are planting in the lives of their children. You can also invest your time in a selfless act like volunteering at a local homeless shelter.

Now, I'm not going to tell you that you will reap a great harvest immediately after sowing a seed. It's possible, but it rarely happens that way. Most of the time, you will go through a rainy season first. The rainy season tends to be the tough times when you just don't know if you can hang on to your dream any longer. It's also the time that you are faced with the hardest and most crucial decisions. When it rains, it pours! However, the rainy season will make you stronger. Think about it. A seed couldn't survive or grow without rain. Similarly, you can't grow without facing those challenges and making those hard decisions.

It's okay to make mistakes. Mistakes don't cancel or stop your harvest. You've got to realize that in the growth process, you will make plenty of mistakes. They're essential for the growth. The important thing is to learn from your mistakes and don't keep making the same ones over and over again. One of my favorite quotes by Dennis Waitley is "Mistakes are painful when they happen, but years later, a collection of mistakes is what is called experience." Just consider a mistake a rainy season, but the sun is shining right in the horizon because you learned from it.

After you sow your seeds and experience the rainy season, it's time to reap your harvest. Just as a farmer is patient during the growth of his crops, you must also be patient while preparing for your harvest. One of my coaching students diligently built his business. He worked long hours and didn't take any shortcuts. He grew to see just how hard it was to run an ethical business in today's world. He was also very active in the youth ministry at church. This guy planted seeds of greatness in every area of his life, and he made it through many rainy seasons when his strength was truly tested. Sadly, he grew impatient waiting on his harvest. He just couldn't understand why his business hadn't skyrocketed yet. His impatience led to him becoming completely miserable and eventually giving up. Instead of preparing for his harvest, he went back to just living a mediocre existence and not expecting anything great to happen.

While waiting on your harvest, you have to have an expectation that it's coming. I have this quote taped to my computer keyboard—"I am expecting a supernatural miracle today." You have to live with a spirit of expectation and constantly prepare for your harvest by speaking daily affirmations. Here are a few of my own affirmations: "I have planted seeds of greatness and my harvest is coming! I see my harvest! I feel my harvest! I expect to receive my harvest today!" You've got to make your affirmations personal to you and what type of harvest that you are expecting. Affirmations are just your faith verbalized. The Bible says "Let us not grow weary while doing good, for in due season we shall reap if we do not lose heart." In other words, don't give up! Your harvest is just around the corner.

Here's another tough question for you. Are you at a point in your life where you know what you want, but you don't know how to get it or what your next step is? That's okay. You don't have to have the whole process mapped out perfectly before you. The first step is the most important step, and that's to make new decisions and stop making excuses. You've made a decision to move forward and pursue your *Why* in life. Now, the next step is to figure out how you will achieve your ultimate *Why* in life. However, you can't develop that plan of action until you can actually see yourself achieving your goals and dreams.

You must create a dream wall in your construction zone. Your construction zone is where you build your business. If you're a network marketer, then your construction zone is likely your home office. If you're a realtor, then your construction zone may be a workspace in someone else's office building. If you're a truck driver, then your construction zone is going to be in your truck. No matter where your construction zone is located, you must have a dream wall. A dream wall is a collection of quotes, pictures, checks, drawings, affirmations, or basically anything that motivates you to achieve your *Why* in life. The walls of my construction zone are filled with reminders of where I'm going in life and the things that I've already accomplished.

One of the most important things that I want you to do is add more pictures to your construction zone. Attend more events and take pictures of yourself at those events with fellow champions and your mentors. If your construction zone is your car, just be very careful where you put the pictures. When my wife, Christie, and I started dating, I stuck our photo in my car near the speedometer. Christie got in the car one day and asked what was burning. I didn't realize that I had placed the photo over the temperature gauge, and I literally blew up my engine. No kidding! I had to trade that car in the next day. So, you see that I am serious about having photos EVERYWHERE!

When you get down and out, just look at your dream board. If you see it, then you can believe it. The world is full of distractions, and it's really hard to stay focused on your dreams. That's why it's so important to plaster reminders all around you. One of my students works in an office setting and is limited on what she can put on her cubicle walls. That didn't stop her! She typed out affirmations and stuck them to her computer. She made a photo collage of her family, goals, and dreams, and put it in a little frame on her desk. Whenever she feels challenged by her JOB, she just looks at down at those constant reminders about where she is going in life.

You have the right to achieve your *Why* and your dream board will keep that in perspective for you, but sometimes those little excuses slip back in the crevices of doubt and fear. The excuses begin to cloud your vision like the fog. Every time you make an excuse, it gets a little thicker. Christie and I often drive up to our cabin in the Smoky Mountains, and there's a reason for the area being called "Smoky Mountains." At times, the fog is so thick that you can't see the taillights of the car in front of you. If you don't follow the caution signs, you will smash into another vehicle or run off the side of the road.

It's the same with that cloud of excuses. Your dream vision is blurred and you can barely see your *Why* in life. At this point, you either take notice of the caution signs and stop the excuses, or you will have zero visibility and smash right into adversity. You don't have to get to this point! If you catch yourself making excuses and avoiding decisions, take a step back and apply what you have learned in this teaching. You now understand excuses are being driven by fear and you have the ability to conquer that fear with your belief.

I don't want to conclude this teaching before covering this question. Why do obstacles, enemies, and unforeseen circumstances come your way? There are several reasons why these negative things occur. First off, recognize that when you're pushing yourself towards the next level of success, you will face adversity. One of my great mentors, Dr. Tom Mullins, often says that, "If you aren't currently in a battle, then you're either coming out of one or preparing for the next one." Adversity is unavoidable on your success journey. If you didn't have to face obstacles in life, then how would you build your strength to conquer the next giant that gets in your way? Allow the adversity to drive you and make you stronger!

One major thing that causes adversity is the junk in your life. The junk I am talking about refers to the people or things holding you back. You can't move to the next level while simultaneously holding onto this junk that's keeping you in your comfort zone. For example, if you attend personal development events on the weekends, but continue to hang out with the same negative friends that don't believe in you, then how can you expect to move forward? Here's another one for you. If your dream is to build a successful business, but the only type of knowledge that enters your eyes and ears is bad television and gossip magazines, how do you expect to promote your belief level so that you can see yourself achieving that dream? It's really not rocket science. You just need to take action and clean the junk out of your life once and for all.

You must begin living your *Why* NOW. Not tomorrow, not next month, not next year. You must begin living your dream NOW! As long as you continue to see your *Why* as occurring in the future, that's where it will always be—in the future. Start living and acting as though your Why is true right now. Who would you associate with? How would you spend your time? In what ways would your life be different? Start today and create an action plan in order to reach your goals and dreams. What sorts of things do you need to do in order to reach those dreams? Write them down and begin to take action on them. Even if you can only think of two things, write those two things down and take action.

More ideas and opportunities will begin to come your way once you make the decision to take action. As the great Martin Luther King, Jr. said, "You don't always have to see the whole staircase. Just take the first step." Take that first step TODAY by making a decision to commit to your goals and dreams.

Once again, decision plus action equals results. To achieve the results that you desire, make the decision to get committed, and take those action steps toward the achievement of your *Why*.

Follow the words of the great Napoleon Hill, who wrote Think and Grow Rich. He said, "If you want to be successful, you must stop making excuses and instead make decisions promptly and definitely. Successful people know what they want and stop at nothing until they get it. They step out in faith and claim what they desire to achieve."

Listen to me. You are one decision away from the next phase of your life, and it's the best phase. It's a more prosperous, successful, and rewarding phase that exists. All it takes is a decision to move forward, stop making excuses, and conquer your fears. It's all up to you! You have the tools to do it, so now just step up to the plate and take a swing. Even if you strike out the first time, in the game of life you have limitless chances to try again. ■

John Di Lemme

In September 2001, John Di Lemme founded Di Lemme Development Group, Inc., a company known worldwide for its role in expanding the personal development industry. As president and CEO, John strives for excellence in every area of his business and believes that you must surround yourself with a like-minded team in order to stay on top of your game.

In addition to building a successful company, John has changed lives around the globe as an international motivational speaker who has spoken in over five hundred venues. Over the past eighteen years, he has shared the stage with the best of the best including Dr. John Maxwell, Rich Devos, Dennis Waitley, Jim Rohn, and Les Brown only to name a few. Recently, John was also featured on Zig Ziglar's webcast. This is truly an amazing feat for someone that was clinically diagnosed as a stutterer at a very young age and told that he would never speak fluently.

John truly believes that everyone needs personal development to reach their full potential in life, and his determination to reach all forms of media with his motivational messages has catapulted his career. John has produced over two hundred fifty products and is an accomplished author of eleven books including his latest best-selling book, 7 Principles to Live a Champion Life. *John has also featured on many television programs and interviewed countless times. As a multi-million dollar entrepreneur, John is one of the most highly sought after strategic business coaches in the world.*

John's passion is to teach others how to live a champion life despite the label that society has placed on them. Through his books, audio/video materials, sold-out live seminars, numerous television interviews, intensive training boot camps, live webinars, websites, podcasts and weekly teleclasses, John has made success a reality for thousands worldwide.

Contact John at www.LifestyleFreedomClub.com, 877-277-3339, or Team@LifestyleFreedomClub.com

Chapter
2

Finding Passion / Life Purpose

I Dare You

by Mike Crow

I **Dare You!** You've no doubt heard this phrase before. It's said when someone is challenging you to do something silly, or worse, something you are afraid of, or even worse a combination of both.

There is a secret to handling this dare that I will share with you before the end of the chapter, as well as one important point to maximize this secret and make it work for you even faster and better.

So, what am I daring you to do? For starters—**I Dare You** to be different—to be willing to do what it takes to push your business or your life to the next level.

Since you are reading this, I already know that you are a little bit different and this is good. However, you need to be warned that others around you will try to make this trait seem like a bad thing. In fact, a common line that I heard as I was growing my business and taking care of my family, or especially worse when I was working for someone else was, "Who died and left you in charge?" or "Who crowned you king?" The answer of course was—no one.

This is important because you need to know that most successful people crown themselves and they do it in a number of ways. You will learn one of the most powerful in just a moment.

Here's an example for you to consider. I remember standing outside "It's a Small World" section at Walt Disney World, with four generations of my family on vacation. I thought I would take a back seat and let someone else run the show. We had agreed we wanted to stay together as a group, so we were trying to decide what do we do next, and then what to do after that. To my amazement, I watched how for 30 to 45 minutes there was a discussion of what to do that unfortunately ended with no consensus or conclusion. It was at this point (as had happened previously many times in my life), that I realized the group needed a facilitator. I took on that role and over the next two weeks we had a great time, and everyone saw everything they could have hoped for and more.

Here is something you may not know about me. Truth be told I would rather be a follower, but I have one rule to taking a back seat approach to life: there needs to be a strong enough leader in charge, someone that I have faith in and knows what they are doing, someone creative, someone with energy and little bit of spunk, someone with courage, someone that I am willing to follow even when I don't understand completely where we're supposed to be going. There are a number of people like me, but there aren't enough of us. So, when you can't find one to take charge, you need to become that person.

There are plenty of people who want to tell you what you should do with your life. Unfortunately they don't have a clue what a totally successful package (business or family) looks like, even more importantly what the dynamics of business **and** family combined should be. This continually becomes clearer as I get older, and even more so why I must be willing to share my knowledge to help others succeed. As you become successful it's imperative that you seek out these leaders and then become one yourself.

How do you determine who these leaders are? **They are successful and help others become successful.**

Now here is something incredibly important to know namely what makes them successful. There are some fairly easy secrets to determining this factor. It is kind of like a magic trick. I am sure you know the type that I mean. Someone shows you a magic trick **and** you say to yourself or maybe even out loud, "Wow!" and then you wonder to yourself how he/she did that. If you are lucky and are persistent enough, you can get them to teach you the secret to solving the trick. In short order you realize how simple it really is.

Dare to be Different

One of the magic tricks you will learn is to be responsible for the outcome of your decisions. Most people aren't willing to do this. For instance, as a small business owner you need to be responsible for the lack of business. The average person wants to blame it on someone or something else, and often the reason behind this behavior is because they don't know how to get people to take action to achieve their goals.

For instance, let's say you have a store. How do you get more people to visit that store? If you have a service business, how do you get the phone to ring more? So, here is one of the biggest secrets that I teach people: understand how to successfully market yourself and your business.

Once you understand this one process you can move anything to the next level both personally and professionally.

I have been told that if you study a subject for an hour a day that in short order you will become an expert in that field. This is true. You will become the expert. So, it is important to study what every business really needs and what you need yourself to move forward with your dreams.

5 Key Points to Better Market Yourself

1) Stay in contact with folks. When I say stay in touch with people, I mean to reach out to them regularly. Are you ready to be shocked? This needs to be done at least once a week and it needs to be something that interests them. This way they look forward to you contacting them weekly. They even will seek you out when this marketing step is done correctly. I coach many people and they are surprised when they see the results of doing

this one step. Here is the good news: you soon get used to doing this and it makes you want to reach out even more.

2) Measure response. Anything measured and reported on expands exponentially. So, when you reach out, you need to see how many folks respond. As you learn more marketing secrets, you will be able to improve this response rate and learn to measure the right things. For instance, home inspectors measure how many new agents send them business to determine if their advertising/marketing plans are working. You will also learn to track how many quotes you are giving and how many sales you scheduled from those quotes. Also, if you measure how many times you reach out, you will improve at this as well.

3) Help others succeed. Help people help themselves is a mantra to live by and it will serve you well. As you learn the power of marketing you can help others become more successful as well. As Zig Ziglar said many times, "You can have everything in life you want, if you just help enough other people get what they want." When you help people, they in turn will want to help you, and when done correctly, they also will be able to help others.

4) Ask for help. When someone says, "WOW! I greatly appreciate your help!" you need to be able ask for what you need to expand your own business. Perhaps a referral, an introduction, a post on their Facebook, an email to other folks outlining the value of your product or service, a donation—the list is endless of what you can ask for. Decide what is reasonable and what will serve you the most. You have basically 60 seconds to make this request and you need to learn the most effective ways to do it.

5) Then do it again. Do this step every day. One of my coaching members sets up a sheet of what to do each day and scores every item from 1 to 10. At the end of the week he totals the score and then the next week he tries to beat it. His business

is growing incredibly fast and so can yours.

So, now you have the secret that will make a difference in your business—Effective Marketing. It is the number one thing that will make you successful. Unfortunately, people might call you names and make fun of you, but in the end many will be asking you for your help or a job with your company.

Learning how to be a world-class marketer and then systematizing the process so it works even when you aren't there is an even better plan. Sounds easy, doesn't it? The only problem is that folks will give you all kinds of bad information and when you try what does work, many will tell you that you are being foolish.

Don't Listen to the Naysayers! Dare to Be Different

One last little secret to make this all easier. Find a mastermind group to share your ideas and goals with on a regular basis. I find monthly meetings are best, but quarterly ones will work as well. I am part of over 10 different mastermind groups currently. Some I lead (facilitate), and some I am a participant. All help me achieve my desires faster and all they keep me focused on the end goal. Trust me – you need a mastermind group.

This is Why I Say…Be Successful and Be Around Those That Are Successful

I help businesses grow their revenue with marketing systems. What I share will not be found in the mainstream or college from where I received a degree in Marketing. What you will learn here is from my years of front line experience.

A little history for you. I founded and managed one of the most successful home inspection firms in North America. I sold this North Texas multi-inspector firm for over a million dollars, and became an area manager for the nationwide home inspection firm that bought it. My area was grossing almost $2 million dollars per year and was experiencing a 40% growth rate the year before I resigned, making it one of the top 5 home inspection firms in the country.

I started coaching home inspectors in 2004 through the

Millionaire Inspector Community where I teach home inspectors how to build their businesses while systematizing their marketing processes and now coach hundreds of home inspectors.

Through adopting my marketing strategies, I'm pleased to say that many people have now built thriving businesses and are achieving the level of success they've always desired. ■

Mike Crow

Mike Crow has 13 plus years experience working and growing retail businesses, and 20 plus years interacting with service companies, teaching them how to make the phone ring more often, getting more dollars per client/customer, and getting them to work with you more frequently. On top of that he helps businesses create passive income streams. whereby money comes in even if they don't work that day. It is one of the most fun things he does.

A National Speaker and Marketing Expert, Mike Crow can make you look like a hero in the eyes of your attendees at your seminars. Whether your event requires a Keynote Speaker or a proven Marketing Expert and Business Coach for breakout sessions, luncheons, sales meetings, you name it—Mike can help make your event a memorable one! For more information visit www.MikeCrowSpeaks.com or www.MikeCrowNow.com.

꧁꧂

From East to West...A Passage of Promise

by Krish Dhanam

*It takes an act of greater simplicity to eat caviar on impulse
than it does to eat grape nuts on principle.*

G. K. Chesterton

L uck has been defined by the optimist as when opportunity
meets preparation. Success has been defined by the opportun-
ist as what you can do in this lifetime based on where you began
and what you began with. Wisdom has been articulated proverbi-
ally by leaders as the correct use of knowledge. Moving from the
abstracts of childhood in rural India to the perceived accomplishments of Western living seem to have in some small dosage all of
the above. Luck, in some measure, coupled with success, seems to
give everyone the appearance of wisdom. Of all who have been
asked to write about achievement and progress, my story may be
the least scintillating since it is filled with gratitude every step of
the way.

Growing up in a sleepy South Eastern Indian town, I watched
the sun rise every morning over the horizon that lined the Bay
of Bengal. I saw ships sail off to far-off lands and wondered if a
voyage of any significance would be in the itinerary of a simple
life. Amidst the chastity of orthodoxy in religion and the endless

worship of all things sacred, I found in life that abstract rituals dominate the dreams of youth and adolescence. The grandeur of the distant was just that—distant and grand. This innocence facilitated in my young heart the need to always wonder. Ravi Zacharias has often said that to an existentialist the wonder is of the present, and to a utopian it is about a mystical time in the future. He adds that a traditionalist is one that longs for the past, but a Christian is the only one who can wonder with certainty that the God of all creation fused the past, the present, and the future. This novelty of what would be in my future was so far from the belief of my childhood that I chose to be a wandering generality.

Like many, I was more a "rebel without a cause" because there was no influence offered with any semblance of causality. If no one offers you a cause to be passionate about, you are content with the choices and chances of your own limited imagination.

One such impulse took me to the northern part of India and there I met and fell in love with my bride of now twenty-five years. I immediately realized the first absolute in my journey and that was that America would be the land where I would pitch my tent. In hindsight, it is evident to me that there are definite signs in every life when certain crossroads appear and a choice has to be made as to which road to choose. If I may be so bold, I claim that such absolutes usually can be affirmed in your own journey if you look at the significant emotional and life-changing events that took place when you were eight, sixteen, twenty-four, and so on. I recommend you take a trip down memory lane and try and recognize for yourself the significance of those events in your own journey. Coming to America when I was twenty-four (about half of my existence ago), was the turning point of when the abstracts seemed to recede and the absolutes certainly appeared.

In the year 1990, I heard a man speak by the name of Zig Ziglar. He gave me many clues in a three-hour seminar, and it is still an event of substantial fascination that a life could be altered by the words of a stranger whose every attribute of living was different and alien from mine. Yet I wanted to be like him and experience the abundant life he was talking about. This course correction that would result in a new identity, not just as a professional, but in a personal and private way, was the turning point of the rest of the story. I went to work for his company in 1991, and using the principles and practices espoused by his writings and teachings, my aspiration to become a teacher of his methodology began. This union that is in its eighteenth year has taken me to fifty-five countries globally and to forty-seven of the fifty states in the continental United States. The ships I saw as a youth sail to abstract destinations had actually transported me in my adulthood to absolute parts of Gods' magnificent earth; they gave me the opportunity to interact with people/groups in the four corners of this world. Along the way I went from reading about wonder to writing about accomplishment. Two books, a corporate title, the forming of a small company and the charter of a ministry have been the rest of the absolutes that make success a worthy pursuit.

The most absolute part of the journey was the third "Q." It is a known fact that man is tri-dimensional and that we are indeed, mental, physical, and spiritual. In the pursuit of fame and the search for significance, most people find the first two "Q's" which are IQ and EQ. The Intelligence Quotient and the Emotional Quotient of functionality give people the will necessary to shape a life and the skill necessary to finance a living. However, the Spiritual Quotient (SQ) is the one in whose absence is the proverbial hole in the soul. When I came to the absolute conviction of the one God who loved me and whose son Jesus Christ was sent to die for me, I felt the chains of separation fall off and every attribute of life change as a result. The story sounds better narrated than experienced, but gratitude fills the heart for the experience of this story that has seen two different lives on two different continents exactly twelve thousand miles apart. I now realize that the abstract of a voyage culminates in the absolute of a distance that we all have to travel. Today as a speaker, writer, evangelist, volunteer, and global ambassador for the Ziglar group of companies, I get to retrace the steps to my origins and try to become an influence for those that will never travel to find their hope. Having shared the stage with two U.S. presidents, titans of industry, captains of enterprise, and the who's who of entertainment and sports, I am comfortable in the certainty of a slum and the uncertainty of a five-star hotel. I am confident that success is manifested when you live by grace and learn to grow in all you do.

Plan with attitude,
Prepare with aptitude,
Participate with servitude,
Receive with gratitude, and that should be enough to
Separate you from the multitudes.

Humility is not thinking less of you. It is thinking less often of you.
Fred Smith Sr.

∎

Krish Dhanam

Corporate Evangelist and Business Philosospher, Krish Dhanam was born in India. In 1984 he finished his MBA and migrated to the US with his bride Anila. Winning a sales contest in 1990 earned him a ticket to a seminar conducted by the legendary motivator Zig Ziglar. This chance encounter would be the catalyst that shaped the next two decades as Krish joined the Ziglar Corporation in 1991 as a telemarketer and eventually became their Vice President of Global Operations.

Through training, teaching, and facilitating seminars all over the world, Krish launched his professional speaking career. As one of only two executive coaches personally trained by Zig Ziglar, Krish has successfully delivered his message of hope, humor, and balance in over fifty countries and throughout the continental United States.

His client list is the who's who of global enterprise and he has received accolades from some of the most distinguished organizations including The United States Army, Christian Dior, Steelcase Industries, Apollo Hospitals, EDS, Texas Instruments, Pepsico, and Energizer Batteries.

Today Krish is the co-founder of a training company, author of **The American Dream from an Indian Heart** *and a contributing author to the book Top Performance written by Zig Ziglar. In the year 2008, following a calling on their heart to do something for their motherland, Krish and Anila formed Mala Ministries.*

The Dhanam's are the proud parents of Nicolas who is eighteen years old and the family makes their home in Flower Mound, Texas, with their canine buddy Jasmin. For more information visit www.KrishDhanam. com, call him at 214.551.9220 or via fax at 972.539.7347.

How to Turn a Sad Moment into a Voice That Uplifts and Inspires!

By James Malinchak

Most people have an inspiration in their life. Maybe it's a talk with someone you respect or an experience. Whatever the inspiration, it tends to make you look at life from a different perspective.

My inspiration came from my sister Vicki, a kind and caring person. She didn't care about accolades or being written about in newspapers. All she wanted was to share her love with the people she cared about, her family and friends.

The summer before my junior year of college, I received a phone call from my father saying that Vicki was rushed to the hospital. She had collapsed and the right side of her body was paralyzed. The preliminary indications were that she suffered a stroke. However, test results confirmed it was much more serious. There was a malignant brain tumor causing her paralysis. Her doctors didn't give her more than three months to live. I remember wondering how this could happen. The day before Vicki was perfectly fine. Now, her life was coming to an end at such a young age.

After overcoming the initial shock and feeling of emptiness, I decided that Vicki needed hope and encouragement. She needed someone to make her believe that she would overcome this obstacle. I became Vicki's coach. Every day we would visualize the tumor shrinking and everything that we talked about was positive. I even posted a sign on her hospital room door that read, "If you have any negative thoughts, leave them at the door." I was determined to help Vicki beat the tumor. She and I made a deal that we called 50-50. I would do 50% of the fighting and Vicki would do the other 50%.

The month of August arrived and it was time to begin my junior year of college 3,000 miles away. I was unsure whether I should leave or stay with Vicki. I made the mistake of telling her that I might not leave for school. She became angry and said not to worry because she would be fine. There was Vicki lying ill in a hospital bed telling me not to worry. I realized that if I stayed it might send a message that she was dying and I didn't want her believing that. Vicki needed to believe that she could win against the tumor.

Leaving that night, feeling it might be the last time I would ever see Vicki alive, was the most difficult thing I have ever done. While at school, I never stopped fighting my 50% for her. Every night before falling asleep I would talk to Vicki, hoping that there was some way she could hear me. I would say, "Vicki I'm fighting for you and I will never quit. As long as you never quit fighting we will beat this."

A few months had passed and she was still holding on. I was talking with an elderly friend and she asked about Vicki's situation. I told her that she was getting worse but that she wasn't quitting. My friend asked a question that really made me think. She said, "Do you think the reason she hasn't let go is because she doesn't want to let you down?"

Maybe she was right? Maybe I was selfish for encouraging Vicki to keep fighting? That night before falling asleep, I said to her, "Vicki, I understand that you're in a lot of pain and that you might like to let go. If you do, then I want you to. We didn't lose because you never quit fighting. If you want to go on to a better place then I understand. We will be together again. I love you and I'll always be with you wherever you are."

Early the next morning, my mother called to tell me that Vicki had passed away.

WOW!

I've often thought a lot about that experience with Vicki and, while it was a sad time for me and my family, Vicki passing away changed my life! She is one of the main reasons I started speaking to groups in the US and internationally, sharing a message of hope, inspiration and encouragement.

Vicki serves as my inspiration as a professional speaker. It's amazing! Out of all the stories I share from the stage in my presentations, more people approach me after to thank me for sharing "Vicki's story" than any other story, success strategy or humorous joke.

That's why I love sharing her story. Not only does it inspire people to live a more thankful and abundant life, but it also allows me to turn that sad moment into a voice that uplifts and inspires.

I hope sharing "Vicki's story" helps you to think about how blessed you are to have good health, safety and peace of life for yourself and your family!

I also hope that it will serve as an inspiration for you that, should a challenging time arise in your life, you CAN get through the challenge and can allow that moment to serve as a message of hope, inspiration and encouragement for others.

Go out and be a voice that uplifts and inspires someone's life... today! ■

James Malinchak

Featured on ABC's Hit TV Show, "Secret Millionaire," James Malinchak serves as an Entrepreneur Mentor to many around the world, while also being a top professional speaker. James also teaches aspiring, beginning and experienced speakers, authors, trainers, coaches, consultants and entrepreneurs how to become "Big Money Speakers." To contact James Malinchak, visit www.Malinchak.com or for more information on attending a live event, visit www.BigMoneySpeaker.com.

Finding Your Purpose and Your Passion

by Nancy Matthews

B y all traditional standards of success, I had it made. My business, a full service title company, mortgage business, and real estate investment company, was thriving. The money was flowing and I was working hard and playing hard. I was taking vacations with my family, owned a beautiful home, and drove a hot red convertible. I was providing a wonderful lifestyle for myself and my two children as a single parent, and creating a great place to work for my employees (who also happened to be family members). Business was booming with opportunities to continue to grow and expand.

It looked like I had arrived. I did all of the things I was "supposed" to do to achieve success and had, by all accounts, achieved it. Why then was there still an emptiness inside me? Why then, did I feel there was something more?

I was a millionaire on paper, but my soul was bankrupt.

I had become complacent and began to feel a slow death burning inside of me. The things that once gave me joy and fulfillment no longer served me. Something deep inside was calling me to dare to be different, but how could I stop doing what I was doing? This was all I knew! I was great at it and it was the source of income supporting myself, my family, and my employees. I wanted to call it quits, close up my businesses, move out of state, and get a fresh start. I wrestled with my desire to break out and do something different, and struggled with the guilt I felt that by doing so would cause extreme hardship for my employees (who remember, were also my family).

It was in this place of internal struggle and complacency that the search for finding MY purpose and passion began. I read books, attended seminars, listened to CD's, and continued searching. By opening myself up to new possibilities and connecting with like-minded people, opportunities to express myself and create a business that would provide more personal fulfillment appeared. The more I explored and searched for the answer to, "What's Next?", the more easily those answers appeared.

My first logical answer to the question "What's Next?" was to dovetail from my existing business and experience to create something new, but similar. Having great success and extensive knowledge in real estate investing, I developed a seminar program to share my "Foreclosure Secrets" with other investors who wanted to create financial freedom through real estate. This new venture brought more excitement and enthusiasm into my life and at first I felt I had found "the answer." The problem was I wasn't very good at speaking in public. Fortunately, my sister, Trish Carr, is a public speaking expert (and also a successful real estate investor), and she showed me how to get in front of the room without my knees knocking, throat closing, and palms sweating.

Trish and I became partners in the Foreclosure Secrets program and were building that business, sharing our secrets with others so they, too, could experience the financial rewards that real estate investing can provide. As a firm believer in always improving my skills and craft, I attended an event called "Seminar Bootcamp." It was there that my next turning point on the path to finding my purpose and passion occurred, and the unfolding of what has now become my mission and my "WHY" was born.

The instructor, Tony Martinez, surveyed the room of 80 people who were aspiring or already successful speakers and he noticed that only 15% of the room were women. He said, "We need more female speakers, women leaders, and women who act like women, not women acting like men. Who in this room is willing to step up to the plate, to take action, and be the forerunner and example for women to be leaders in their own right, not women trying to be men?" In that instant I felt something deep inside of me stir. It was like an electric shock to my system and I jumped out of my seat and shouted, "Me, Me, Me!" His call to action hit a chord inside of me that I didn't even know existed. Until that moment I didn't know how important it was to me to take a stand for women's empowerment. In retrospect, I now see that it is something I've always stood for, believed in, and acted upon. I just didn't recognize that I was doing it.

The significance of this event is not that I am now the leader of the Women's Prosperity Network, an inspiring and moving female leader and public speaker group sharing the message for women to acknowledge their greatness, and providing ways for them to tap into their inner strength and share it with the world. The significance is the spark that was ignited to create the momentum for the continuous unfolding and fulfillment of my personal mission. The chord that was hit when Tony spoke from the front of the room was the chord of "What's Next?" and set me on the path of looking inside myself instead of outside to find my purpose, my passion, and my personal power.

Finding your passion and your purpose is a journey, not a destination. Through different times and phases of my life my purpose has been changed, and I know it will continue to grow and evolve. I remain open to this exciting evolution and have learned to trust my intuition to guide me on the journey.

Since you're reading this book, there are a few things I know (or think I know) about you:

- You are also on a journey of self-discovery, empowerment, and personal fulfillment.
- You are willing to invest in yourself to explore and experience

the life of your dreams.

- Your dreams are "Big Dreams" that go beyond material possessions and that you are committed to making a difference, not only in your life, but in the lives of others.

You are a "Visionary with Guts!"

You are a heart-centered and passionate person who has a vision and the guts to go for it. I have been dubbed "The Visionary with Guts" and I know that within each and every one of us is a visionary, and that the "guts" comes from having people to support, encourage, and guide us in fulfilling our vision. The "guts" comes from being willing to face the obstacles and challenges which will no doubt surface, and move beyond them with the conviction and commitment to fulfilling your vision. The "guts" comes from being willing to look inside yourself to find your purpose and your passion, and knowing that success is a journey, not a destination.

I offer you the following *7 Simple Steps to Reveal Your Passion, Purpose & Power*. These are the steps that I used (and continue to use) to reveal my passion and purpose. I invite you to be patient with the process, to remain open and aware, and to listen for those moments, those turning points which occur that ignite the spark within you that touches upon your true purpose, passion, and personal power.

7 Secrets to Revealing Your Passion & Purpose

Secret 1 – RESERVE TIME FOR YOURSELF

It all starts with YOU. Reserve time for yourself. Give yourself permission to spend at least 15 minutes each day just for you (30 minutes would be even better). If that seems impossible, request a copy of *7 Sacred Steps to Balance*. [Send your request to Nancy@WomensProsperityNetwork.com]

Secret 2 - HAVE AN "INSIGHTS" NOTEBOOK

Get a journal, notepad, or even one of those old-fashioned black and white composition books. This is where you will start to write down your notes, ideas, insights, thoughts, and dreams. Not a writer? No worries. The exercises we suggest are easy and don't require you to be a literary genius. If you can write a "To Do" list or jot down ideas on a post-it note, you can do these exercises.

Secret 3 - RECOGNIZE WHAT MAKES YOU HAPPY

As you go through your day, start to recognize those times when you're feeling happy and what you are doing at those times. Write down in your notebook the things you do that make you happy. This list will grow over time. Just be sure to capture at least one thing each day that makes you happy. It could be as simple as giving (or getting) hugs, taking a long, hot shower, singing songs along with the radio, walking the dog, etc.

Secret 4 - SCHEDULE "HAPPY TIME"

Be sure that you schedule "happy" time in your day and your life. From the things you discovered in Secret 3, make time to do at least one of those things each day. Using this simple step, you'll be living a happier life.

Secret 5 - IDENTIFY YOUR HEART'S "SOFT SPOT"

This is the beginning to revealing your true passion and purpose. Answer this question, "If all my financial needs were met, my **S.E.X.** needs (**S**afety, **E**ssentials and **X**tras), and I had so much money that I **had** to give some away, who would I give it to and why?" Another way to look for this is to determine where is your heart's soft spot? Do you want to help children? Women? Animals? Taking the time to look at what you would do for others if you weren't so busy taking care of the basic needs for yourself and your family, will allow your passion to be exposed.

Secret 6 - GET SPECIFIC, LIST THE DETAILS

Now it's time to get specific. Think again about your soft spot. Who do you want to help or serve? What are some of the ways that you can help them? For example, a person who wants to help women who are victims of domestic violence may want to start a shelter for them, to develop programs to help them get out of their situation and start a new life. What is your heart's soft spot? Where do you think there's a need to be filled and what can YOU do to help fill the need? This is when you will not only state what it is that you want to do to help others (as you did in #5 above), you will also list the details of what you need to do to make it happen.

Remember that revealing your passion and purpose is a process and it will likely take some time. Be patient and kind to yourself, but be persistent. Do Not Give Up! To have your dreams and goals come through you must keep your focus on them consistently.

Secret 7 - WRITE IT DOWN AND SAY IT OUT LOUD 7 TIMES A DAY

Once your passion and your purpose are revealed to you, write it down on a piece of paper. Then make 3 copies and put them clearly where you'll see them on a regular basis. On the bathroom mirror, on the refrigerator, on the dashboard of your car – wherever you'll see it often throughout the day. Read it regularly, at least 7 times per day. Thoughts become things! The more you think it, say it, and believe it, the more it will come to you.

Bonus – Secret 8 – BE OPEN AND ALERT

Keep your eyes, ears, and mind open. Now that you have identified, stated, and affirmed your passion and purpose, opportunities to fulfill your hearts desire will appear. I'm sure you can remember a time that you wanted a red car, bought a red car, and then suddenly more and more cars on the road were just like the red car you just purchased. Did it happen that lots of other people wanted the same car at the same time you did? Or was it just that once your red car was identified to you, it became part of your thinking and visual awareness? You've identified your passion and your purpose (just like you did with the red car). Be alert. Pay attention to what you hear on the radio, TV, new people you meet, conversations, magazines, and in other media.

Fulfilling your passion and purpose, will happen. It is truly magical and it is your life's purpose to fulfill your mission. Remember, you are a "Visionary with Guts!" ■

Nancy Matthews

*Nancy Matthews is an Executive Business Consultant, an International Speaker and an Author, with over 25 years of experience. She has shared the stage with some of today's leading experts on business and motivation and delivers keynote presentations at Chambers of Commerce, ABWA, Jafra, and many other corporations. She has been featured on NBC6 several times and is known as the "Visionary with Guts" for her willingness to blaze through challenges and obstacles and to turn adversity into advantage. Her captivating book "Visionaries with Guts" is an anthology with 30 "Visionaries" who have all moved beyond their fears and frustrations to achieve success and they share their strategies and secrets so you too can enjoy life as a "Visionary with Guts." The creation of that book, from concept to publication within 2 short months is yet another demonstration of her "Gutsy" dedication to fulfilling her dreams and serving others. She is the founder of Women's Prosperity Network which provides online resources and live events where women committed to excellence mastermind and achieve breakthrough results. She has owned and operated multi-million dollar businesses and now uses her gifts of word wizardry, business savvy and an intuitive understanding of people to support others in growing their businesses. Her Magical Marketing Makeovers are just that… *Magical* and bring her clients great success and prosperity. For more information visit www.WomensProsperityNetwork. com, www.VisionarywithGuts.com or contact Nancy via email at Nancy@ WomensProsperityNetwork.com, or phone at 954.727.9700.*

❧

Our Passion Can Change Our Course

by Terri Schmidt

Twenty plus years ago I moved to Nashville, Tennessee to pursue a career in the country music industry after a life-long passion for music and entertaining. Performing at Opryland USA in Nashville, productions for such industry leaders as Ford and American Airlines, as well as Christmas Shows for people of all ages, helped to fulfill that passion. Making people smile and laugh was truly a love of mine. I met incredible people and many doors of opportunity were opened to me as I was privileged to travel to Cuba, Panama, and Honduras through the Department of Defense to perform for our troops serving in Central America. It was while in Honduras visiting a location site in which our troops were building roads for the farmers in the mountains, children began to run down the hill to meet us. They were running through the hot dirt with no shoes on their feet. It was at that moment I began to pray that God would allow me to return to Honduras on a mission trip to serve and provide for people in real need. I now had a new passion. The desire to learn praise and worship songs in different languages as to honor the peoples in their native tongue took root in my heart.

The last 20 years I have been married to an incredible man, Harry Schmidt, my knight in shining armor, and an NHRA Hall-of-Famer. We have two incredible daughters, Hillary, 18, and Hailey,

17 years old. All three are the absolute loves of my life. As a family we tremendously enjoy extensive traveling across the country in a motor coach. Alongside our travels through the U.S., we also have had the amazing privilege of venturing as a family to the Amazon River and *an answer to my prayer* of traveling down to Honduras on mission trips.

While on a trip to Honduras in March of 2009, I was asked by a fellow Honduran missionary team member to begin praying that God would provide a new vehicle for him and his family. Rodolfo is a husband and father to a family of 6, and was transporting his family in a two-seat small flatbed pick-up truck. He truly needed a much larger vehicle. I told him I would commit to begin praying along with him that God would provide the vehicle. Before leaving Honduras that trip, I inquired on how much it would take to provide a truck for Rodolfo. I learned that $10,000 would afford a nice used truck in Honduras. I began to pray and later learned that Rodolfo had been praying for new transportation for over 15 years.

Upon returning home to the U.S., I received a phone call from a dear friend that I had worked with in Nashville, TN. She wanted to share with me a new business venture that she had just invested in which there was unlimited earning potential. My husband had recently retired from 20 years in the jewelry business as a wholesale jeweler entrepreneur. I did not need to start a new business, as my husband had provided for the needs of our family when he sold his company and decided to retire to begin traveling with us. We had just returned from Honduras, so my thoughts were not on what I needed personally after hearing, witnessing, and living the real needs of the peoples in Honduras. I declined partnering with her until I received a text message from my friend that changed everything. The message read: "Do you know any folks that might be interested in my business? We have a new $10,000 bonus on the table. Cindy."

A few mornings later, while reading the scriptures in my quiet time, I remembered the cost of a new truck for Rodolfo. I glanced across the table at a Habitat for Humanity Magazine that had caught my attention. A printed quote from the very first Habitat volunteer read, "Even in success the victory is never finished. Your **gift** is an **investment** that **never stops earning**." I immediately picked up the phone, called my friend, and said, "I am in!" With no business knowledge of the company or experience in running one, I took a leap of faith and jumped in with both feet without looking back. The bonus incentive now applied to me as well and I had an opportunity to fulfill my commitment.

The window of qualifying for that bonus came and went and I soon realized that God was showing me that I was going to have to work hard to acquire the funds to follow through to see my goal take fruition. Several months went by and I understood that work, commitment, and being stretched out of my comfort zone in order to grow my business would take time and determination. Perseverance in training, goal setting, and personal development would be the key to expanding my business that in turn would increase my level of pay. I continued in my devotions and scripture reading which lead me to recall a verse that I had read many times before, but now brought a new meaning and became prevalent in my life. Proverbs 3:28: *"Do not say to your neighbor, Go and come back, and tomorrow I will give it, when you have it with you."* I could not ask my friend Rodolfo to wait any longer. My family and I made the donation and set the purchase process in motion to get him his new truck. I decided that I would now work intently to return those funds to our family account as soon as possible.

Once again God opened the door for my daughter and me to return to Honduras in March of 2011. We had another incredible experience of witnessing God in action and spent time with the children at La Finca Los Ninos Orphanage in Valle de Angeles. We also returned to Valle de San Francisco and ministered there as well. As our trip came to a close I rejoiced with Rodolfo and his family as well as Pastor Danilo, who also received funds for a vehicle for his church ministry. God divided the $10,000 and provided two vehicles for two incredible families and ministries. As we were rejoicing with the Pastor, I asked him to pray for my husband who was scheduled for surgery upon my return to the U.S. I was not aware that as he was praying, he too was scheduled for surgery on the *same day* as my husband for the *exact same procedure*. Two hearts were instantly bonded: two nations, tongues, and families became bonded for eternity. God is so amazing.

The month of March seemed to be a short month for striving to reach a milestone goal I had placed before myself within my company. With travels to Honduras, my sweet husband's surgery, and taking my daughter on a college experience, time was of the essence. But again God intervened and brought Molly, my new business partner, into my life. God gave me the opportunity and I had to initiate with the follow through. Together we reached our goals and set my personal business team up for success.

Only a God Like You

Passion, desires of the heart, and setting goals in motion with a steadfast belief system, will take you to places in your personal growth that you can't even begin to imagine. You will start to accomplish milestones that you did not think were possible. Awareness of God's presence and the ways in which He speaks to us is critical. Your business presentations will become powerful and you will be able to expand and explode with enthusiasm as you witness the phenomenal changes that can occur. Opportunities are presented to us and we must then take the leap of faith and zero in with a laser focus. Keep your eyes on the prize that is encompassed in the clouds and lined with the threads of His Majesty. You will be amazed at the things you will be able to accomplish.

My Nashville experience opened the doors to some incredible opportunities that led my life in many different directions. I have amazing memories of great moments and incredible adventures. Being a wife and a mother is truly my greatest accomplishments. Partnering with the doctor's that created Proactiv Solution® and riding the huge wave with them in their new business venture into Direct Sales with Rodan + Fields Dermatologists, is one of the greatest decisions I ever made. I am passionate about seeing lives changed as a result of what this company has to offer. In April of 2011 I was pleased to be recognized as the *First Level V Leader* in the State Of Texas with *Rodan + Fields Dermatologists*. Just further proof that combining faith with determination and hard work does prove to be fruitful. ■

Terri Schmidt

Terri has performed with such recording artists as Steven Curtis Chapman, Little Texas, Diamond Rio, Out of The Grey, Skip Ewing, and comedian Chonda Pierce before they were in the spotlight. Sharing the stage with Lee Greenwood, Minnie Pearl, and Brenda Lee was incredible. Traveling to Central America and performing for our troops was the highlight of her career. The last 20 years she has been busy being a wife and mother of two now teen-age daughters and a zealous volunteer to many causes. Terri recently launched a new business in unfamiliar territory and is extremely excited to nurture and grow her company in order to follow her passions. To find out more about Terri and her business, visit http://tlcskincare.myrandf.com, email her at T8140@aol.com or call her at 214.435.0208.

Life Coaching Can Help You Cope After Loss

by Roberta Stack-Constantino

Have you ever dealt with stress or loss? Stress at work, with your kids, loss of a loved one, a marriage, job, independence, or health? I bet I can honestly say that everyone reading this said yes to at least one or two of these statements. Well, I can say yes to them also.

I am the youngest of four children, with a brother who is the oldest and two older sisters. In 1981, I had just spent my first week in college and came home for Labor Day weekend. That weekend was the worst weekend in my life. I came home, we got caught up on each other's news, and then went off to do our own thing. My oldest sister and her husband were taking both sets of parents out to dinner to tell them they were going to have a baby, the first grandchild on both sides of the family. My brother, other sister, and I went our separate ways to see old friends etc. My parents came home and told my sister and me the great news about the impending arrival of a new niece or nephew and we were all so excited. We couldn't wait to tell my brother Gary, but he never came home! We waited and waited, looking out the front window watching for him, but nothing. Finally, we all went to bed saying we'd catch up with Gary in the morning.

My parents received a phone call around 3:30 a.m. from the hospital asking if they were the parents of Gary M. Stack. They told them that there had been an accident, and they should come to the hospital. We knew then that the news was not good. My parents left for the hospital with heavy hearts. I told my sister that he was killed in a car accident and I told her where it had happened. Several hours later my parents returned home telling us that Gary was gone. He was killed in a car accident about a mile from where I told my sister it happened. One of the saddest parts was that he was almost home when the accident occurred.

This was the most horrible feeling in the world I had ever experienced. How could this happen? Why did this happen to him, to my parents, to me? I was in shock, disbelief, angry, and sad. I think I felt every negative emotion at that point. My brother was my idol. I did everything he did, and we did almost everything together. How could I go on without him? Maybe if I did something good, God would bring him back. Why would God take him of all people? He was one of the good guys!

I'm sure that many of you can relate to these feelings. We all go through them in different ways when dealing with loss or stress. Well, it took me awhile to get over the loss of my brother. Back in 1981, there weren't many books out there on coping with the loss of a sibling. They were all psychology based and very depressing to me. All I could think of was that I was crazy. There also weren't support groups for dealing with loss, at least none that I had heard of or could find. We also did not have computers or the internet to go online to get help. I had to figure out how to cope with this all by myself. Nowadays, you can go online and find a support group and chat with professionals, and also, perhaps more importantly, to others who have gone through the same type of loss that you have.

I always knew that I was meant to do something different, something big that would help others. I have always been one who helps everyone. I love it! So, one day while sitting with my father in the hospital waiting room while my mother was getting breast cancer surgery, my father and I had a long talk. We discussed our lives and what we would have done differently and what we wouldn't have changed. I talked about all the things I had tried to do that just weren't "IT." Then, as we talked, I just blurted out, "I'm going to write a book on coping with the loss of a sibling. I'm going to call it *Coping with the Loss of a Sibling: I Miss You, Gary*, and have other people's stories in it also. There will be stories of hope and inspiration in the book to help others." All I can remember is my father looking me straight in the eye, grabbing my hand, and saying, "Now you've got it!" From that day on, I have not stopped. I did write my book called *Coping with the Loss of a Sibling: I Miss You, Gary*. I started giving seminars on Coping with Loss, Coping with Life Transitions, and started my business, Life Guidance and Solutions, in which I am a Life Coach who focuses on helping others to live the life of their dreams—the life that they deserve.

I've learned that coping is a process. It is something everyone does in their own way. Each of us has our own personality and we handle situations very individually. That is something we need to remember. Some talk about their loss, some don't, yet I've found it is best to talk out your feelings. Getting your emotions out is a wonderful healing process. If you can't talk to a family member or friend, try your religious leader, a life coach, or a counselor. People are out there to help you, if you will allow yourself to be helped.

This is where life coaching can come into play. I wish coaching would have been around when I was going through the pain of losing my brother. I definitely would have used a coach to help me to cope and move on with my life! Coaching can give you an objective person to talk to about what you are going through and feeling. Coaches are not counselors, psychologists, or psychiatrists. We are coaches. We ask purposeful questions to help you to find what is best for you. We basically help you to help yourself to live the life you want, how you want to live it. We help you to figure out what goals you have for yourself and how you are going to reach them. This knowledge is very important when dealing with loss in order to move forward with your life. If you have lost a loved one, you may now have different life roles than what you had before. What are these new roles and what can and should you do with and about them? How are you going to do them? What do you need in your life in order to be able to carry on? These are some of the questions I ask when working with people in the coaching process.

This is just a portion of the things I have started doing to help others. All stem from the things I have learned, not only from the loss of my brother, but of my grandparents, a good friend who was killed in a car accident a month or so after my brother, coping with divorce, and being a full-time parent to two girls. I also have had to learn how to process my father suddenly dying a year and a half ago, and dealing with my mother who was an alcoholic all of my childhood and well into my teen and early adult years. From dealing with her exacerbation of dementia after my father died to putting her in a nursing home, dealing with my mother and sister having different types of breast cancer, coping with my daughter who basically had a nervous breakdown after my father died, and needed much emotional care…and the list goes on.

I could have taken two different paths in dealing with these plus many other issues. I could have hidden my head, started to drink, and/or taken drugs to numb my feelings, or not accept anything, become introverted, and not deal with any of it. Or, I could face everything head on and start accepting what was going on. I realized I had to choose the latter before I could move on, so I did exactly that. The way I did this was to find a positive in any given situation. For my brother, I had to think about him. He had lost his girlfriend whom he wanted to marry to cystic fibrosis. He was never really happy after that, so I felt he was with her after his death, in a place where HE wanted to be. With my friend who died shortly after my brother, it was a little harder as I suffered two losses so close together, but I just had to realize she was meant to do something up in heaven. I didn't know what, but I truly felt there was a reason, and I may never have an answer that I felt comfortable with, so I just feel that she was needed elsewhere. With my dad, I knew he wanted to be with my brother. He was tired and sad. We buried my dad on his 81st birthday. My brother's birthday was November 14th and my dad's was November 11th. We always celebrated them together, and now they were able to celebrate together once again. That made me happy.

When you accept a loss and move on, it doesn't mean that you forget the person or situation. You never forget the person/situation, nor should you. I talk to all my loved ones all the time. I express my gratitude TO them and FOR them every morning before I get out of bed and every night before I fall asleep. I thank God for allowing me to have had them in my life at all. The real tragedy would have been to not have ever known them. I am grateful for them and for what they taught me. I am who I am because of what I have learned from each and every one of them, and each and every stress and loss that has occurred in my life. Now what I do is to help others to feel that same sense of gratitude. To accept, move on, and grow from each and every loss. As difficult as a loss may be, you can still learn and grow from it. It just may take a little longer to cope, accept, and realize your gift. I understand you are probably thinking, "This woman is crazy! I can't do this!" Well, I'm not, or at least I don't think I am. Anyway, it is possible if you let it be. You are in control of your life and your thoughts. You need to think positive thoughts, as what you think is what you believe. I read in one of Anthony Robbin's books, "What you focus on you believe!" Think about that. What are you focusing on this minute? Then think how that thought is playing a role in your life.

As you can see, you can live a happy and productive life after suffering a loss. I am living proof. You may just need a little or a lot of help, but that is okay. There is nothing wrong with that. That is where coaching comes into play. Give yourself permission to grieve, to cry, and to live happily again, and you will if you believe it and allow it. So, go start coping and start LIVING! ■

Roberta Stack-Costantino

Roberta has a 25 year history of working in the Occupational Therapy field, which has helped her to cope and deal with loss on a personal and professional level. With her experiences of loss, life transitions, and coping in a positive manner, she is now helping others to do the same. She is now a Life Coach and offers seminars and workshops. She wrote Coping with the Loss of a Sibling: I Miss You, Gary, to help others to deal with the loss of a sibling. She is also now extending her life coaching services via Skype and teleseminars. To contact Roberta, you can mail her at P.O. Box 41471, Brecksville, OH, 44141, call her at 440.759.9178, or visit her website at www.LifeGuidanceAndSoultions.com.

Chapter
3

*Overcoming Fear
and Procrastination*

❧

Overcoming Your Fears
The Journey to Faith
by Jeffry S. Angelo

It is documented that there are 536 known phobias in the human psyche. The one that surprises me the most is euphorbia, the fear of hearing good news. Really? What could have possibly driven a wedge between you and good news? Caution! If you have this phobia, save yourself and stop reading this chapter now because this is just the beginning of the good news.

Mind you, I am not a psychologist. I do not possess a degree in the inner workings of the mind from anything other than thirty years of intense leadership in the field of herding cats, or to be clearer, the Santa Claus and Easter Bunny photography business. As you may imagine, I do have some experience in assisting with Santaphobics or those who fear Santa Claus. These are generally 16 to 24 month old toddlers who spend the better part of the year dreaming of their much anticipated visit to see Mr. Christmas, Santa Claus, or also known as the Big Guy.

They sit in a one-hour line, (if they are lucky), fidgeting, sucking down juice boxes, and eating every snack imaginable that can fit into a 16-quart baby bag, only to get within two feet of this larger than life childhood hero and experience unimaginable fear. If you can believe it, I have seen 50 year olds with this fear. Believe me—a 50 year old Santaphobic is not as endearing as a toddler suffering the same fear, but it is just as real no matter what the age.

First, we need to understand exactly where fear comes from. Why does fear cripple us? How do we rise above this very powerful emotion when courage is needed? Like any good tool, it takes practice to overcome fear, but surprisingly, the cure is much simpler than one might imagine. What I am about to share with you will help to illustrate how to begin to get to the other side of your fears.

Mark Twain once said, "Denial ain't just a river in Egypt." Start by admitting to yourself that you tend to freak out quite easily and that it is time to quit feeding the fear monster. Then begin to open your mind, and more importantly, your heart, to changes that begin with these five important steps.

Acquire knowledge. Prepare and plan. Forgive yourself from failures in the past. Wait to worry, and have faith.

Acquiring Knowledge

It is tough to look on the bright side when you are stuck in the dark.

The lack of knowledge is extremely self-defeating and yet it is the easiest fear to mitigate. I do not know who coined the phrase "ignorance is bliss," but they obviously had never been on a road trip without a map!

There is nothing blissful about ignorance. However, it is inexcusable. Ever hear of a thing called Google? I remember when I got my first computer with a 56KB landline modem. HEAVEN! Now I could open up that little baby and surf the net. Of course, in those days, it was like trying to swim for Olympic Gold in a pool of mud, but who cared? You can literally find anything on the Internet. The accessibility of information is everywhere. So, we can strike the lack of knowledge off the list. When we become informed, we find enlightenment. *Fear does not reside in the house of enlightenment.*

Preparing and Planning

A good plan brings the future into the present so you can do something about it now.

When NASA sends the Space shuttle up in space, they spend thousands of hours planning every aspect of the journey, but, really, how hard can it be? They have done it more than a hundred times. Just light it up and get on with it, right? Wrong! No matter how many times they go at it, there are still thousands of points of failure, and all must be addressed before the ship leaves the pad because once the countdown starts, it had better go right.

If it can break, how, when, why, and where will it happen? Every point of failure is a point for a contingency plan. Leave nothing to chance, even if it is as simple as picking the kids up from school. Always have a backup plan and you will lead a fear free life. Good planning makes elusive dreams come true. Good planning with contingencies eliminates anxiety. A good plan removes barriers before they even exist. A good plan is a fear killer and is as refreshing to the soul as a cold glass of lemonade on a hot summer's day. Plan and relax.

Fear of Failure

Fear lasts a day but regret lasts a lifetime.

Fear of failure is the most prolific fear of all. We have heard all the stories of the great inventors of our time like Steve Jobs and Donald Trump. One invents the coolest gadgets on the planet and the other reinvents himself almost daily. What a concept. Do you think that they have experienced the fear of failure? You bet they have. However, it is the way we embrace this fear of failure that separates the pretenders from the contenders.

Embrace your failures. There are nuggets of treasure in every one of them. Forgive yourself of the outcome and resolve yourself to dig for the gold that is hidden in the experience of your failures. None of us desire to be wrong, but when you take the risk, you open up unimaginable opportunities.

Ask yourself, "What is the worst thing that can happen if I fail?" In reality, hindsight is not 20/20 but 50/50. And no matter how much you think you know, it is the variables that have the potential to derail you. So, the sooner you get accustomed to making mistakes and building off of them, the quicker you will transform the "fear of failure" into the "friend of failure."

Failure is the down payment you pay for success. When you bite the bullet you can become a shooting star. The next time someone tells you that failure is not an option, just say, "You are right, it is not an option; it is an opportunity!"

Nothing is Ever As Big As It Seems

Wait to worry and you will always be worry free.

Have you ever had a big presentation to make and you want it to be perfect? You practice and practice until the big day comes only to find that everything is upside down. On the flight to your presentation site your printed materials were eaten up in the luggage monster, and you are running fifteen minutes late due to a truck that just dumped its load on the freeway. To top it all off, the projector in the boardroom is not working. OMG!

This is your life and it's all that you have ever wanted. But all at once the opportunity is crashing from circumstances beyond your control and fear is crippling you. Then realizing that you have no choice, you muster up just enough strength to sheepishly claw your way to the front of the room, too afraid to make any excuses. I mean, who would believe it anyway? So, you begin without the projector, without any written materials, and with only a vague memory of what you had planned. You hit the highlights. After all, that is all you can remember. As you start, heads begin to nod as if there is genuine interest. You have forgotten at least two thirds of your written presentation, but somehow, late or not, materials or no materials, they love it!

Twenty minutes ago you were gripped with fear and now you are just amazed. *Nothing is ever as big as it seems no matter how big you blow it up.* So, when you are inclined to panic, try this very simple exercise: wait to worry!

Faith...The End to ALL Fears

Fear knocked on the door. Faith answered and, lo, no one was there.

For those of us who have suffered through unbearable loss, it can be paralyzing. No words of comfort or any of life's simple pleasures can replace the loss of a loved one. Only time and enlightenment will comfort this very real and painful reality. Fear is a by-product of the grieving process, but it must take a back seat to the most important choice we can make in this life—having faith.

A dear friend of mine had suffered the most unimaginable tragedy one can fathom. On September 12, 1995, his only son was kidnapped by a family friend for ransom and brutally murdered. After a yearlong friendship with this incredible man, I finally mustered up the courage to ask a question that had been on my mind since the day we had met. "How do you EVER trust anyone again?" He graciously leaned into me and uttered one word, *"Faith."*

You see, he got it. He understood that if he allowed his grief to paralyze his path he would never rise above it. He conquered grief and loss one prayer at a time. One week after sharing the most important word in life for overcoming all fears with me he died suddenly, but his legacy was a testament to all who knew him.

Courage is born of faith. Whether it is the loss of a job, a marriage, or a loved one, faith is the most important tool in overcoming the fears that can paralyze us. You have a Daddy, a loving caring, giving Father in Heaven who feels your pain. He will provide liberating comfort when fear grips you. All you have to do is prayerfully ask. He is there for you...always.

We are all just transients in this world and time is short. So, stop fearing and start living!

> *Faith is being sure of what we hope for and certain of what we do not see.*

Heb. 11:1

Start today to live in faith, not fear. ∎

Jeffry S. Angelo

Jeff Angelo is a leader with a passion for encouraging others to greatness. Jeff mixes humor and wisdom throughout his organization by sharing stories of hope and planning with a purpose. He has found the sweet spot of life in the heart of Christmas' most famous jolly 'ol self; just be a giver. As President & CEO of Trend Concepts Unlimited, Inc., he manages 350+ mall event photography promotions, has trained over 4000 Santa's, 18,000 cast members, and captured over 15,000,000 holiday memories.

Jeff has been featured on ABC's 20/20, USA Today, Wall Street Journal, CNN, and numerous other state and local television/radio and news/print publications.

His mentors include Zig Ziglar & Truitt Cathy. To contact Jeff, mail him at Trend Concepts Unlimited, Inc., 26069 Springer Cemetery Road, Hockley, TX 77447. You can also email him at Jeff@Sepianet.com or reach him via his office phone at 936.372.3111, Ext. 103, or on his cell at 832.256.5555.

The Power of Lists
to Supercharge Your Life

by Tony Rubleski

I t challenges me when I find myself thinking about or seeing people conspiring each day against their own greatness because their inner thoughts are out of purposeful alignment. In addition to this problem, "misery loves company" type of thinking and behavior is now celebrated, packaged, and sold on hundreds of daily talk shows and TV programs up and down the dial. Millions of people are addicted to and negatively influenced by it.

The ratings and market for negative based media and information speaks volumes about our society and the priorities, (or shall I say lack thereof), that people give to their time, talents, and ability to positively serve others. While a few people who read the last sentence may feel that this is arrogant or mean spirited, that's fine with me. If it offends someone and wakes them up to take a better look at their own life to improve it, versus simply complaining and watching other's lives, then I'm on track with this chapter.

It's amazing these days how we have millions of people who claim they can't find more "time" to learn a new skill, find a better job, or start a part-time business, but still spend multiple hours each day in front of their computers or flat screen TVs frittering away their skills and potential greatness. With modern technology, creature comforts, and unlimited amounts of competing options for free time now available, it will become more of a challenge to resist distraction, unless you deliberately change and grow your thinking, habits, associations, and beliefs about success and achievement.

For example, it's amazing to me how many people obsessively watch other people's lives through reality based TV shows. Now, full disclosure, I watch a show or two myself, but I'm more concerned with those who watch several hours each day and then complain how good or bad their own life is based on what they see. Most of these shows are seductive, interesting, entertaining, and cleverly scripted and edited to weave the illusion of being 100% real.

Many loyal viewers use these shows as an escape and never realize that they're taking their own valuable life force, meddling into other people's drama, instead of creating and living their own dream. If this describes you, then I'll tell you up front to please snap out of this mental trap and illusion. This chapter will be like a healthy dose of smelling salts to wake up your mind to not just a different way of viewing the world, but positively acting upon it. Here's a bold proclamation to set the tone of where we'll journey over the next few pages:

It's time to shut off the negative shows in your head, computer and TV screen, and start scripting your own life for excellence and achievement.

We have too many people watching and waiting, when they should be focused on investing more time designing and carrying out their own plan! To help set the stage for scripting your own life for the better, we'll explore several forms of lists that are essential to create, review, and take action upon each day that will serve you well.

The Goal Isn't To Bring You Down, But To Get You To Rise Up and Reclaim Your Inner Genius NOW, and Without Further Delay!

I've seen many people in my own life, including my own father, turn the initial death sentence of six months or a year left to live, into a **live life to the fullest sentence**. I'll explain. They treated these remaining days like gold, without inhibition, and the key phrase: without fear! What if we all lived this way? What a very different world it would be. I sense that many people would treat each day with a passion and intensity that would marvel and inspire themselves and those around them.

Father time is strange indeed. When we're children life moves at a crawl, and when we're adults it begins to pick up speed like a snowball rolling downhill. We cannot go back in time and rewrite or live in the past. Nor should we allow the two thieves known as regret and guilt to haunt and steal our valuable time known as the present. An untrained, negative, and beaten-down mind filled with regret and fear is much more dangerous to success than most people realize or can even imagine.

The Honor List

The names and dates are unfamiliar to most people, but to me they are pivotal markers and turning points in my destiny and journey.

Stan Rubleski	1984	Age: 46
Robert Austin	1985	Age: 19
Dan Hutchinson	1993	Age: 21
Craig Shriver	1995	Age: 22

Four names, four years in time, four major people who left an impression on my soul and present state of how I look at motivation and action. Like a bright, burning, orange flare in a pitch black forest, each one of them grabbed my soul and uniquely changed my destiny in ways that no one could imagine or possibly link together.

Frozen in Time, But Never Forgotten

The years and ages of Stan, Robert, Dan, and Craig represent the year they exited the game of physical life. Their life clocks here on Earth burned out quickly and far too soon. Two of them passed from cancer and two of them were involved in freak accidents.

While many people these days obsessively worry about retirement and multiple "what-if" scenarios as to what they'll be doing when they turn 50, 60, or 70 years of age, this was not an option for the four people I've listed. Unfortunately, they never had the chance to fill their minds with such trivia, for their life force was snuffed out at relatively young ages. It's okay and healthy to dream and think of the future, but sadly, most people obsess and worry relentlessly about a future date or marker in time that may burn out before they even get there. Each day thousands of people are notified that their life will end soon, while others get no warning at all.

The List of Four Exercise

I'm a big believer in creating and using lists to get things done quicker and with less stress. Yes, for men it's wired into our DNA. This next exercise is designed to make you appreciate the life and talents you might be taking for granted at this moment in time. I'm going to have you create a very different type of list that you may have never thought about making, and move it from your head into the physical realm via pen and paper. Be prepared: this will also conjure up many strong emotions from your past.

If we sat down over a cup of coffee and I said to you, *"Write up your own list of four people who've passed on and how they positively impacted your life,"* what names and reasons would you put on the list and why?

I want you to do this right now. Take a few minutes and write their names on a piece of paper or in the spaces provided here.

1. _____

2. _____

3. _____

4. _____

The ages and dates of the names on my own list of four serve as a stiff reminder to me that death is a part of our existence, and can come in the prime of life with some advance warning and often when we least expect it. The goal here of creating your own list of names is to remind you to deeply think about your own life, appreciate it, and look at each day as a gift to be celebrated and lived fully even during the hourly ups and downs. If you made up The List of Four for yourself, welcome to the club. I now urge you to honor these people in your life by going after your dreams and passions with a renewed sense of urgency.

A second question: *Is your current life honoring them or would they wonder why you're squandering it?* This isn't an easy question to ask, yet alone think about. However, it's essential for you to dig deep within your own life story and answer this question. Again, the goal is to allow these people who were in your life to inspire you to rise up and cultivate your inner genius.

Look, every human who's ever lived, past or present, has made trade-offs. I believe true-life balance is one of the biggest myths still being packaged and sold across the radio and TV talk show circuit to society. It's sexy to talk about "work and life balance," but achieving it is not easy. Many times when we're in flow or actively pursuing a big goal, creative chaos will take over and mess with balance. It will happen, trust me. It's important to continually gain perspective and work towards recognizing that a short-term imbalance is required to help us in the long-term to see our dreams take shape.

Finally, let me ask you a third question that few people, especially those in business, rarely if ever stop and slow down to ask themselves: *What really drives and inspires you to play the game?* Each of us gives up most of our waking hours and valuable life force to work for someone else or to build and pursue our own enterprise. There are no time-outs in life, so let me ask once again, what really drives you to play the game? In the sped up, digital, interruption based, media overload society, many people are getting bogged down in distraction and worry about what others are doing, thinking, saying, writing, or watching, instead of focusing on themselves.

If you aren't motivated, focused, and truly sold on your dreams for the life you're living and designing for significance, then how in the world will you pull it off and attract the people and resources needed to carry it out? When these ingredients are missing, a mental tug-of-war takes place and sabotages many good intentioned people.

Let these exercises serve as an action guide to discover new lessons you can learn to cultivate and grow your inner genius. You and I are travelers on the journey called life. We may have never met, but I can tell you one key thing we both share: We want more from life, we often see the positive potential in others, and we're curious to discover ways to keep growing.

Two Other Essential Lists to Serve You Well As You Reinvent and Reclaim Your Inner Genius

#1. Gratitude List
#2. Goodbye List

Gratitude List. In my written journal I have a list of 78 things I'm grateful for each day. It's in the front of my journal next to my goals, and covers a wide range of items including God, family, health, friends, travel, music, past accomplishments, and on and on. When you create your own gratitude list and review it each day, or pull it out when you're having a challenging day, you'll be amazed at how it will change your mind-set for the better.

"Reflect upon your present blessings, of which everyone has many; not on your past misfortunes of which all people have some."
– Charles Dickens

Goodbye List. Very few people do the next written exercise I'm about to describe. I urge you to do it immediately. It will seem unconventional and strange at first, but please stay with me and resist reading past this part as it's essential in helping you remove negative past associations, anger, and guilt within your own unique life story.

In the spaces below, I ask that you take a minute or two to write down the name(s) of those who have caused grief, stress, or undue mental anguish in your past that you need to forgive and remove from your mental space. To jog your mental archives here are the most common areas to draw from: family, career, school, religion, friends, and acquaintances.

Name(s):

_____ _____ _____ _____

_____ _____ _____ _____

_____ _____ _____ _____

Now, I need you to quickly grab a piece of blank paper nearby. Take the names you've just listed and write them on the sheet of paper. Now, take the freshly written page of names, review the list carefully, and say out loud: *I forgive each of you; it's time to move on with my life. Goodbye.*

After you've done this, pick up the paper and slowly crinkle it into a ball and throw it away.

Here are several reasons this is such a powerful mental exercise:

- You free up your mind and let go of old negative emotions such as guilt, anger, and fear associated with these people.
- It's helps you to create greater clarity and focus in pursuing the new, empowering goals and outcomes you seek within your life.
- When you forgive others, which is not easy for most of us to do, you'll realize that we all are flawed human beings and the

negative emotions we once held not only wasted our precious time, but blocked our ability to achieve and attract better people and outcomes into our lives.

• By writing these names down, speaking out loud the statement I just described above, and physically taking action by rolling the paper into a ball and throwing it away, we anchor into our minds the seriousness of our intentions.

Reprinted with permission from the book, "Mind Capture: How to Awaken Your Entrepreneurial Genius in a Time of Great Economic Change" ©2010 Lightning Strike Press. ■

Tony Rubleski

Tony is currently the president of Mind Capture Group. His message is designed to help people 'Capture' more minds and profits.

His second book in the Mind Capture series *titled* Mind Capture: How You Can Stand Out In The Age of Advertising Deficit Disorder *went #1 in three different business categories with Amazon.com and received stunning reviews from a wide range of leaders in marketing, sales, psychology to academia, entrepreneurs, and multiple New York Times bestselling authors. In late January of 2011 he will release his third book in the series titled,* Mind Capture: How to Awaken Your Entrepreneurial Genius in a Time of Great Economic Change!

His work has been featured in various media outlets ranging from Bottom Line Magazine, The Detroit Free Press, the FOX TV network, to CNN Radio, NPR, and Entrepreneur Magazine Radio. In 2009, NWA in-flight magazine, World Traveler, featured Mind Capture *as the Business Pages selection of the month.*

He writes regularly for several magazines, blogs and trade publications on sales, marketing, and motivation related topics. He's also a faculty member at the U.S. Chamber of Commerce where he teaches in the target areas of marketing and technology topics for chamber and association executives. In addition, he's the editor and creator of A Captured Mind monthly newsletter which also features audio interviews with top authors, business leaders, and other well-known newsmakers. For more information visit www.MindCaptureBook.com.

Chapter
4

Goals

Can't Never Did Nothin'

by Kay Loree Case

D o we go through life not knowing whether we are just living a life orchestrated by others, or do we have choices to make along the way? Think about this for a minute. What choices have we made and what outcome was directly related to those choices? Many of us have a variety of life experiences. Our parents shaped part of our reality, whether consciously or unconsciously. The rest has been shaped by us. Armed with self-beliefs from the past, we bring these beliefs into the future. I have realized that there are many possibilities for outcomes. Every decision I've made through happenstance or through effort has determined my destiny. But then, what in my past had shaped my present and future outcomes?

Humble Beginnings

I grew up on a small farm in northwestern Wisconsin, the youngest of five children. My dad thought that children were to be seen and not heard. Very few signs of affection were given to us by our parents, a behavior passed down to them by their parents. I spent time in the fields and woods dreaming of bigger things. I was resourceful in my dreams, creating castles out of brush, riding horses with Roy Rogers, and pretending I was Dale Evans. My father worked in a meat-packing plant in South St. Paul, MN (two hours away), and came home on weekends. Most of my mother's life was spent farming with my brother, who was seven years my elder. I was not expected to go to college. I was expected to get married and have babies like my mother and my older sister. My mother's biggest fear for me was that I too, would get pregnant out of wedlock like she and my sister. Somewhere along the way, my mother realized that life was passing her by. In the 1960's she made a very uncomfortable change; she got a job working in Minneapolis as a nanny and later as a sorority housemother. She left me and my brother to milk the cows and farm the land. Believe me, it was not easy to milk cows and then go out on a date. Those years were the foundation of being responsible and knowing that there wasn't any use of complaining, I just had to do it. When I said, "I can't" to my mother, she said, *"Can't never did nothin'."* I have remembered that throughout my life as I have had my share of trials and tribulations. Remembering what she said still stays on my mind, to the point, in fact, that I don't think twice about most decisions now. If it feels right, I know I have to go through that door of opportunity. After all, if I don't, I would always wonder, "What if I could have made a difference in someone's life?"

My Early Journey

I graduated with 48 other kids from Shell Lake High school in 1967 and then went on to college. I married my high school sweetheart at the age of 19, and graduated in 1971. I considered myself a "B" student. I wanted to go to medical school, however, my mother didn't think I could accomplish this extraordinary goal. You see, to her doctors were way above my station in life. It is the only time that my mother didn't encourage me. I believed her because she was my mother. So, I settled on getting my Bachelor of Science degree in Medical Technology. My first job was in a medical laboratory for a large regional hospital. I worked hard and had an appetite for knowledge. Within six months of starting my career, I was offered a position as supervisor in Hematology and related departments. I became an expert. I succeeded because I worked hard and tried to be the best I could be. This paid off as I was next offered a supervisory position in Immunology. In this new field of study even the tests were not commercially available at that time. I accepted that position even though it entailed the supervision of staff in a field that I knew nothing about. Have you ever supervised individuals who knew more than you do? It was tough, but it made me remember my mother saying, *"Can't never did nothin'."* I fostered a team approach and soon we were developing tests that were on the forefront of medical research.

In 1977 a prominent researcher from Yale University spent a three-month sabbatical in La Crosse, Wisconsin, to study a virus that killed two young children who were bitten by mosquitoes. The mosquitoes were found to be infected with a virus, later named the La Crosse virus. When the researcher came, I realized that even though he had a PhD in virology, I had knowledge that he didn't have. I knew how to design immunologic tests from the ground up.

I began to develop complex tests used to confirm exposure to infectious disease. This led to a flurry of exciting new diagnostic tests which could identify other infectious diseases. Additionally, this knowledge gave me the opportunity to start publishing. In the beginning, we collaborated in publications, and eventually by 1982 I started my own 10-year research study to determine why some children got encephalitis (an inflammation of the brain) from the viral exposure and others did not. At that time, Immunology was a relatively new field of study in the medical field. Why then did they name me as the principle researcher and grant me $20,000 (a lot of money in 1982)? Research foundations typically fund PhDs or students working to obtain a PhD. Remember that my highest degree was a Bachelor of Science in Medical Technology. I was funded because they knew I had determination. They had faith in my conviction that with the help of my laboratory staff, we could do this research.

When my medical director, co-workers, and I conceived this area of study, we wondered why some exposed children had little more than flu-like symptoms while others became gravely ill. We hypothesized that there was a mechanism where the immune system could collaborate with our genetic makeup to recognize, attack, and present the infective organism materials sooner to the immune system. Two years after we brought this theory forward, a paper was published by other researchers describing how our body recognizes dangerous infective foreign material versus organisms that are normally present in our body. Eight years later, we finished our study and confirmed there was a genetic disposition for having complications of encephalitis. Believe me, it was our curiosity and common sense, rather than any innate genius that helped us make this discovery. Once again, the doors of opportunity opened and I walked through. These efforts led to the education of the public sector on the avoidance of mosquitoes. Through our efforts, we were able to identify the areas of highest occurrence of the disease, aid in earlier recognition, lower the number of encephalitis cases, and most importantly, eliminate La Crosse virus related deaths.

If I would have said, "No I can't" and if I hadn't become involved, the researcher would have taken his information back to Yale, published his research in some journal, and our community would have never benefited. Did my effort require a PhD? No, it was my conviction, passion, and knowing that I could, which catalyzed the next events. I was part of the leadership that made it possible for children in the area to be made aware of the danger. Our grass root efforts shaped the process for educating members of the community.

I failed to mention that I while doing this, I continued with the responsibilities of my real job as supervisor of the Immunology department. Oh, yes, I proved that *"Can't never did nothin'."*

The Road to Oxford

Self-talk can be a blessing or a detriment. We can say that we can't do something and this gives us an excuse to avoid the hard work that may be required to do the alternative. I became interested in Lyme disease when cases of this infection started to emerge as a medical concern within the La Crosse area. After my dog was diagnosed with Lyme disease, I started to wonder about my own symptoms of chronic headaches and hip pain. At that time, the Center for Disease Control (CDC) was distributing the Lyme disease organism to only a select number of laboratories. I obtained the organism from the Wisconsin State Laboratory and began creating my tests. I collected a bank of specimens from well-documented cases of Lyme disease. This specimen bank of known positive serums became an international resource for manufacturers who were developing tests to identify persons with this disease.

This effort was very time consuming. I had a family life that was also demanding. I lectured across the State of Wisconsin to educate medical providers and community members. A virology researcher that I had worked with previously on the La Crosse virus, knew I was going to a microbiology meeting in Stockholm with my colleagues to present our work. I was surprised when I got a call asking me to stop off and speak to his colleagues at Oxford University, when at the time the British knew little about the disorder as it was not prevalent there. I couldn't believe I was being asked and I was scared to death to even consider this. Do I say "I can't" or do I say "I can"? Then the self-talk started. This was Oxford we were talking about. I was just a laboratory technologist. Fortunately, he reassured me by reminding me that I knew more about the subject than they did and that I would do just fine. So, I remembered my mother's wisdom and decided that if I blew it by having stage fright, swallowed my tongue, or developed a new case of stuttering, what difference would it make? So, I spoke at Oxford University.

At the beginning of my presentation, I kept telling myself over and over, "I know more than they do." You know what? I did just fine. My first 10 minutes were a little rough, however, at the end of that hour presentation, I felt this farm girl from Wisconsin had accomplished a most amazing thing! So, if you believe in yourself and summon the courage to open the doors of opportunity, your world will open up to new possibilities. You can accomplish amazing things if you remember: *"Can't never did nothin'."*

The Expansion of Life's Opportunities

So, as a farm girl, who grew up both physically and mentally in that rural environment, I never lost sight that I wanted to be a doctor. At the age of 48, I was again presented with another door of opportunity to go through. I decided to put this decision in God's hands and applied to a Physician Assistant (PA) program at the University of Wisconsin-La Crosse/Mayo Program which accepted only 12 students. I was the 13th on the list of candidates. If anyone dropped out of the program I would be next in line. Was I disappointed for not being selected? Somewhat, but it was also a relief as I now had an excuse for not becoming a doctor rather than saying I can't. Then four days before the program started, someone had to decline their position in the class. Wow! I had four days to tie up 25 years of work in the laboratory, prepare my family for this 27-month sacrifice, and find financial support. I could have said no as my negative self-talk abounded. Could I really do this? After all I hadn't been in school for so many years. The PA program is very difficult as it is essentially an accelerated medical school curriculum. My mind wanted to say no, but then I figured that if she would still be alive, this time my Mom would have encouraged me: *"Can't never did nothin'."*

So, I practiced as a PA for five years and since this career is very similar to being a physician, I realized my dream of a career that is close to that of a doctor. In addition, four years ago, I was offered a position of an Assistant Professor at Nova Southeastern University in the SW Florida PA Program, where I currently teach. Has my journey finally been fulfilled? Not by a long shot. I feel that we all can expand our life's dreams into reality, even further than we can imagine. Each and every one of us has opportunities. Why? God wants us to expand our horizons and be successful, because through our success, we touch other lives in ways we can't imagine. So, what about my horizons? Well, I was offered an opportunity to write this chapter and I believe that I will have many more opportunities in the future. And you know what? I will always remember what my Mom said: *"Can't never did nothin'."* And you know what? I know **I CAN!** ■

Kay Loree Case

Kay Loree Case earned a Bachelor of Science degree at the University of Wisconsin-La Crosse / Mayo Clinic Physician Assistant Program and a Master of Physician Assistant Studies degree from the University of Nebraska. She currently holds a faculty position as Assistant Clinical Director and Assistant Professor at Nova Southeastern University. She has published 13 peer reviewed journal articles and two book chapters. She lectures for Nova Southeastern University, Florida Academy of Physician Assistants (FAPA) symposiums, as well as internationally to include University of Oxford, UK. She has two children, three grandchildren, and lives in Naples, Florida with her husband. She enjoys her pets, kayaking and golfing. To get additional information on Kay Loree Case, visit her website at www.CantNeverDidNothin.com. You can also contact her at 239-274-1025 (office) or 239-272-1198 (cell).

Thinking Outside Your Box

by Tish Gray

D o you ever make decisions in life, whether with a relationship, your career or money based solely on logical thinking rather than listening to your inside voice? Do you ever have that "gut" feeling and not know whether it is right or not? Based on society, regardless of where you are from in the world, there are social norms, the culture, if you will. These social norms shape us in many aspects of our life. Conforming is sometimes more important in the culture than listening to that inner voice that may contradict the social norms of where we are from. Educating on financial money management so that you may live a more fulfilled and less stressed out life is a passion. In addition, teaching people how to use their logical thinking in regards to managing their money while listening to their inside voice is where to begin.

Thinking outside your box is about all of life and creating your reality in conjunction with using your reasoning. A common tool with people who are analytic, like myself, is using "pros/cons" lists. This allows me to make a decision based on which side is "weighted" differently. For instance, recently I was thinking about buying a new car. I used a pros/cons list and realized that it would be better to keep my older Lexus, even though my heart wanted a "new shiney" car. Thinking outside the box in this situation involved not only the logical list, but also thinking about how car payments, or writing a big check for a liability would "feel". My inside voice (in addition to my pros/cons list) both said "KEEP THE OLDER CAR

THAT IS PAID OFF!"

It is good when these two ways of making decisions agree... but what if they disagree? For instance, say you have been in a relationship for years (or married for years) and the relationship seems to be drifting further apart than together. A divorce attorney that I am friends with uses the triangle in his relationship classes to explain in a relationship, you can either grow together (the point of the triangle) or grow apart (the base of the triangle). Either way, the relationship grows, it is just which direction. When deciding whether to stick out the relationship, you may seek an outside advisor through therapy, try to work through the issues yourselves, or you may choose to call it quits. When making a decision such as this (which I have done a time or two seeing that I am divorced), make sure that you are first discussing with the other person so that all of the information is on the table, then seek counsel along with your pros/cons list. Finally, make sure that you are listening to your inner voice.

You may ask the question, how do I hear what my inner voice is saying? In the world, American culture (where I am from) specifically, there is so much information, that we often received data overload. Additionally, in American society, and in my opinion throughout the world, we have become a world of "I want now". Not wanting any type of deferred gratification, causing many conflicts in our relationships as well as our internal compass of ourselves. It is amazing to me, that the DSM IV recently did not include narcissism. My question to you is, do you think our culture in America actually is breeding, accepting and condoning being the center of your own world above all else? If you think the answer is no, just stop reading here.

If you think the answer is yes, like I do, we are becoming a culture that is spreading the world of "ME!" across the globe, as opposed to thinking of others, and the affect our actions have on others.

When I was younger, I could not see beyond what I wanted "right now". Whether it was a nice dinner with fine wine, a new outfit, shoes, or a relationship that may have been toxic and completely wrong for me, I didn't want to wait to get any of these things. This did not end well with some of my relationships as a teen and in my early 20's. Additionally, the "it feels good" mentality just was not working for me. The first time I recall hearing that inner voice shouting at me was on Semester at Sea, during my last year of undergraduate. I was living in San Francisco, the playground of anything you want whenever you want it, second only to Las Vegas in my mind. It was great! I lived for the nightlife and for "fun". When is was about time for me to go on Semester at Sea, I had to get to Vancouver, Canada for the boarding of the ship and took the Green Tortoise (the Green Tortoise was a hippie bus filled with mattresses to fit as many travelers as possible) all the way up the coast line. Upon reaching Vancouver, I was so excited to embark on the adventure of a lifetime, where we were to go to 13 countries while circumnavigating the globe. We were off, to Japan, Hong Kong, China, Malaysia, then to India. Before we were to get to each country, there was professor that would get in front of the 600 students on Semester at Sea and tell us a bit about the country, how to say a few phrases and what "not to do". This trip was years ago and some of the areas we were visiting were not developed yet. Before we got to India in the southeast industrial port, they told us two things:

1) Do not travel by yourself.
2) Do not use public transportation (unless the train).

The year before, there had been 3 students that were killed when a public bus ran off the road. The faculty on the ship did not know until well after the ship had left India. So of course being 20 years old and knowing everything, and being quite confident in my travel expertise, I was determined to travel by myself. I had made a promise to myself; if I only spent time with other mostly American students, I would not be able to fully experience the culture I was immersed in for a week at a time. Additionally, there was a student on the ship from India and told me of an ashram, Sri Aurobindo, in Pondicherry that was only about 3 hours from our port. That was all that I needed to hear before deciding I was to adventure there…yes, by myself.

As soon as we docked, I made my way passed all of the docked ships in the industrial area until reaching the main street…

resembling nothing I had ever seen before. There were rickshaws everywhere, along with automobiles, motor-scooters, and bikes. The traffic was a kind of congestion I had never experienced before. As soon as I saw a taxi, I was off to a women's clothing store where I would buy traditional garb and cover myself from head to toe. Aside from the blue eyes and western tennis shoes, I looked like a local (in my mind). My next stop, to a public bus station, once again by myself. I was about to head to Sri Aurobindo in the country on a 3 hour or so bus ride (it is worth mentioning for about $1.50 at the time).

After about 3 hours and sights that I had never seen before, we came upon the most beautiful white buildings I had seen. Sri Aurobindo was a self-contained community that was built by the French. Upon check in, I was informed I was there during silent time, meaning I could not talk to any of the other guests! Yikes! The only thing I liked doing more than traveling was talking! This was going to be a challenge, especially because I was staying for three days! Not wanting to give up, I was quiet. The first day, all the chatter between my ears was killing me! It was sheer torture to not be able to share all of the experiences of this foreign culture! The second day, I noticed the chatter and "noise" going on between my ears started to subside a little. The third day, I found myself in a new place...I found peace and was able to stop the chatter. Once I stopped the busyness of life, and just got quiet with myself, I actually felt a weight lifting from my shoulders (metaphorically). I was able to see who I really was; the way I was created; and also, peace and contentment with who I was for the first time in my life! I had new eyes! I could see things, differently. I understood things I didn't understand before, saw people the way they were created and realized WE are all the same. This new found contentment, I translated into "happiness". It was Anne Frank who said,"We all live life with the same objective, to be happy; our lives are all so different and yet the same." During that weekend, I confirmed this for myself, and also understood the wisdom in Frank's quote. It does not matter what country we are from what language we speak, or what color our skin is, we are all the same. We are all just searching for "happiness".

That trip to India and the experience of finding myself would be a monumental change in the course of my life. Well, OK, it was a "life changing" trip. What does this have to do with thinking outside the box? If I had done what I was told (the 'safe' thing to do), the ashram would have never been a part of my life experience. In order to listen to my inside voice, what I needed at the time in order to grow (which was very uncomfortable at the time), I had to think outside the box and shut out all of the outside noise. In my life, especially American culture, has become so 'busy'. Anytime you talk to a family member or a friend…when you ask how they have been, what do they say?…"Busy". We have become so "busy," that the simple things in life, like taking some quiet time has gone to the wayside.

If you find yourself answering "I have been busy" every time someone asks you how you have been doing, it is time to have some quiet "me time". Yes, you have a career, yes you have kids, pets, spouses…but we are letting ourselves drift into the mundane and not thinking outside the box at all!

Here are some action steps that you should take…not next year, but in the next 3 months for yourself.

1) Take at least 5 minutes (it does not sound like much, but it really is) for yourself and start a journal (gratitude journal preferably) for just one month and see how you feel.

2) Make your list of things you enjoy doing, but never have time to do…even if you are only able to do one of those things in a 3 month period, give yourself permission to enjoy life sometimes.

3) If you have a "New Year's Resolution" you have been making for years and keep up with it for the first week of the year, COMMIT to yourself to do one of those starting not in 6 months but TODAY!

4) Start to dream again! Do you remember as a child having "play time" or using your imagination to make up fun stories? Well, start to dream again and think about what your life is missing and set a goal even if it is a 5 year goal…is there a place you have always wanted to visit? A show you

wanted to see? A new language you wanted to learn? Go back to school? Have your own business?

5) Start tracking these things for 6 months...yes, it seems like a long time...but DO IT! Not tomorrow, next week or next year...TAKE ACTION TODAY! ■

Tish Gray

Tish Gray is an Author, an International Speaker and Financial Consultant/Coach. Tish is also the owner and founder of Holistic Planning Institute, LLC.

Tish presents on financial literacy and money management as well as inspirational and motivational messages. She believes to live a holistic lifestyle, you have to reduce stress and get educated on your financial well-being in addition to your other life spirals. Since money issues are one of the "stressors" in life, financial education and well-being is essential to live a harmonious and enriched life. Financial Education on a corporate level and on an individual level is Tish's passion.

Learn more at: www.HolisticPlanningInstitute.com

༶

It's a Phenomenal Life

by Howard Partridge

I'm originally from "L.A." (Lower Alabama!). I grew up on welfare in the city of Mobile, AL. There were 7 of us kids crammed into a little 600 square-foot shack. The roof on that house was so bad that every time it rained we had to get out the pots and pans to catch the leaks!

The house was perched on concrete blocks so there was no slab or full basement. It had a teeny-tiny shower (no bathtub) that barely had enough room to turn around. One day my stepdad got in, and it fell through the floor to the ground! We propped it back up with tree-stumps which created a gap between the shower floor and the rotten sheetrock. If the soap was dropped and bounced the wrong way, it would be in the dirt, UNDER the house!

We *invented* soap-on-a-rope!

My little mama somehow fed us on a hundred dollars a month from the welfare department, and I still remember getting Christmas presents from the social workers. My real dad left when I was only a year old and I didn't get to meet him until I was 15. The only time I recall seeing him was at my maternal grandfather's funeral. I must have been about five years old at the time.

As I stood on the sidewalk of the funeral home with my family, a long black limousine passed by and someone said, "There's your father". The back window of the car was rolled down on his side and I got a glimpse of him. When he saw us, he placed a handkerchief over his face. He must have been so ashamed. Little did I know that he would become a significant part of my life later on.

How does a childhood like that usually turn out? You become a pot-smoking, hell-raising teenager. And when you have a stepdaddy named Hollis Odell who drives a truck by day and is in a honky-tonk band by night, things eventually go bad.

When I was 18 years old, things went very badly one day. My stepfather and I got into a fight. I ran out of the house and just before he slammed the door, he yelled "And don't EVER come back!" By the way, I DESERVED this.

This event turned out to be the best thing that ever happened to me. I had NO money. At the time, my older sister was visiting my real dad in Houston, TX, (who I had met only twice at this point). My friend and I scraped up $39.95 for a Greyhound bus ticket to Houston. I wasn't real sure my dad would actually take me in, but I knew my sister would find a way.

When I stepped off that bus in downtown Houston, I literally had 25 cents in my pocket. No bank account. No credit card. That's all I had to my name. My real dad was there to pick me up and I lived with him and his new family (who I became very close to) for about a year. I made sure to patch things up back home in Alabama too. Although both daddies are now gone, I have a great relationship with both of my families today which I am very grateful for.

After working a few odd jobs in Houston, I became a professional waiter, wearing a tuxedo no less, and worked in high-end restaurants where we did flaming tableside cooking. I learned how to make a lot of great dishes at the table - Steak Diane, Pepper Steak, Caesar Salad dressing from scratch, Hot Spinach Salad, Bananas Foster, Cherries Jubilee, and many more. Setting stuff on fire inside was very cool indeed!

During my years as a waiter, I learned a great deal about the customer service experience, but I really wanted my own business, as I've always been an entrepreneur at heart. As a kid, I had cut grass, picked up pine cones, sold stuff door-to-door, and did anything I could to make money.

As I waited for the last table to leave each night, I scratched out business ideas on my waiter's pad, but I still had no money to speak of. I made just enough to pay the bills.

That's when I met my future wife. Denise Concetta Antionette Pennella. Now that's Italian! I went to New Jersey to get married to Denise and when you marry into an Italian family, you don't get wedding presents like dishes, toasters, and blenders. Instead, you get CASH!

We got $3,000.00 in wedding money and while we were in New Jersey, there was a friend of the family who was my age (23 at the time), driving around in a little red Mercedes convertible. I said to myself, "I want to know what THAT guy does, and I want to know if it's LEGAL!"

Turns out he owned a legitimate business, so, as soon as I got back to Houston, I spent all of our wedding money to start a business. Let me tell you, my wife was really thrilled about that!

I started my first business out of the trunk of my car, and I still own that business today. Over 13 long years I built it up to where I was making about $30K per month. I was making good money, but I had become a slave to the business. Everything revolved around me. I couldn't go on vacation without the appointment book or spending much of the vacation time solving problems over the phone.

If you're a small business owner and you have been in business for awhile, you know what I mean.

Two Big Secrets That Changed My Life Forever

My mentor, Bill Beckham, would come to my office about once a week to talk and pray with me. As he observed how involved I had to be in every little detail of the business, and how dependent it was on me, he recommended I read The E-Myth Revisited by Michael Gerber.

That book changed my business and my life forever.

I took a week off and went to my favorite place in the world, Destin, FL, and sat on the beach and re-created my future. The first secret I learned was how to build a turnkey business—one that operates just as well without you as it does with you. I learned how to work on the business instead of just in it as The E-Myth says.

The second secret I learned is that the only reason your business exists is to help you achieve your LIFE GOALS. You went into business for yourself because you had a dream of having more time for your family—a dream of doing WHAT you want WHEN you want. Instead, you sometimes feel like a slave to the business.

That's what I felt like. I was literally a prisoner of my own making. Don't get me wrong, I LOVED serving my customers, and doing the technical work of the business, but now I saw a different picture. I saw that I could have a turnkey business.

My business partners and I began working on our systems and that little business skyrocketed to grossing almost $3 million per year! And the best part is that it is turnkey now which means I don't have to be involved in the day-to-day operations. I now have a staff of 27 that run my companies for me.

In 1998, I launched my training company Phenomenal Products, Inc., and began teaching my systems to other business owners. Over the past decade I have had grown a phenomenal training business and had the pleasure of having some amazing people on my stage including Michael Gerber (author of the book that changed my life), as well as world famous Zig Ziglar.

It's a PHENOMENAL Life!

In the classic film "It's a Wonderful Life", Jimmy Stewart's bank had it all, but it collapsed and he was on the verge of jumping off a bridge to end his life. Little did he know that he had a Guardian Angel assigned to him and many wonderful people that loved and cared for him regardless of the circumstances.

We live in a fallen world and we never know what trial we may face tomorrow. Learning to respond properly to the circumstances we face is one of the first keys to living a phenomenally successful life.

One of my best friends was Ray Davis. Ray suffered from MS for many years. The last 10 years of his life he couldn't even get out of bed as his arms and legs were stiffened in place by the disease. Even his fingers were permanently gnarled up and inflexible. As he lay there in constant, agonizing pain, he could move only his lips. If you didn't know Ray like I did, you couldn't understand his garbled, slurred speech. I was glad that I could because Ray's purpose was to encourage everyone who came to his bedside.

Regardless of his condition, he wanted to know about your life and how you were doing. He always glorified God and was so thankful for the little things. My "problems" seemed small after leaving Ray's bedside. I was grateful just to be able to walk to my car.

The last time I saw Ray alive was late at night in the hospital. I was the only one there and the room was dark. A nurse had come in to service the room. Ray wanted to pray for her. In the last hours of his life, his concern was for someone he barely knew!

Ray used what he had. He may not have been able to help anyone physically, but he was able to make a difference with what he did have: his heart and his mind.

Gratitude

You may not feel that you have much to be grateful for. Maybe you have tremendous problems. Maybe your future doesn't look bright. I want to introduce you to a mental process that I think will serve you well. It has not come easy to me, but I now realize that when I use it, I am able to focus on what is truly important.

Some years ago I was introduced to a wonderful ministry called Living Water International (LWI). LWI drills wells across the world in places where clean drinking water isn't available. I learned from them that almost ONE BILLION PEOPLE on the planet don't have access to clean drinking water! I discovered this is the #1 killer on earth!

How is that possible? That's 20% of the planet! I quickly learned to be more grateful for what I have. If you live in America, you have so much to be grateful for. Being able to just flip a switch for light, access to clean drinking water, and warmth from the cold when you need it. We have the freedom to worship and the freedom to pursue our dreams. The freedom to grow a PHENOMENAL business that will take you places you never dreamed possible and to bless more people than you could ever imagine.

"Of all the "attitudes" we can acquire, surely the attitude of gratitude is the most important and by far the most life-changing."
— Zig Ziglar

Be grateful for the little things and your mind and heart will be opened to new possibilities for your life. Otherwise, you will stay stuck in your own prison of pity.

Every day when we wake up, we have a choice of what to focus on. When your "problems" begin to fill your mind, or you begin to become overwhelmed with the duties required for today, stop and replace those thoughts with gratefulness. Begin to think about what you do have. Thank God for your freedom. Thank God for everything you have in your life. Be grateful for the little things and you will see your attitude begin to change and you will make a difference in other's lives as well.

"Finally, brethren, whatever is true, whatever is honorable, whatever is right, whatever is pure, whatever is lovely, whatever is of good repute, if there is any excellence and if anything worthy of praise, dwell on these things."
— Philippians 4:8 New American Standard Bible

■

Howard Partridge

Howard Partridge, president of Phenomenal Products, Inc., helps small business owners and professionals build predictable, profitable, turnkey businesses that allow you to live the life you went into business for in the first place. Howard's live events have featured Michael Gerber, Zig Ziglar, Tamara Lowe, and many other best-selling authors. Howard has been featured on Ziglar's Success 2.0 Webcast, and has a published article by McGraw Hill Professional. He has owned 8 companies all together and has members across the world. Howard delivers his proven solutions through information products, webinars, live seminars and coaching. For more information visit www.HowardPartridge.com or mail him at Howard "Phenomenal" Partridge, Phenomenal Products Inc., 808 Part Two Drive, Sugar Land, Texas 77478. You can also reach him via phone at 281.634.0404.

Chapter
5

Life Balance

The Power of Coaching Up

by Bryan Dodge

M en and women business owners value leaders who demon-strate an enthusiastic and genuine belief in others and who strengthen their will to succeed. Leadership is all about developing human talent. There are a number of companies that I have spoken to have actually renamed their human resources department the "human talent department." Those companies get the concept that leadership needs the heart and skill of a coach. Leadership is less about command and control, and more about coaching people to live up to their potential.

Yes, businesses hire a manager to increase sales and control costs associated with the outcome or production of business. However, people do not want to be managed; they want to be coached and mentored. Coaching is far more productive and longer lasting. Coaching is all about focusing on the person's talent and not so much about the production of the job description given when hired. Coaching gives a business the advantage of creating a culture that stands strong during tough times. If businesses focus on enhancing their staffs' talents, I believe their outcome will greatly improve. Coaches focus on supplying the means to achieve, and not on the fear of employees losing their jobs. It is the title of coach that helps you express optimism for the future with a firm walk in life. It is a coach's focus that helps support people's growth with a new level of disciplines. Legendary football coach, Lou Holtz, said, "Discipline is not what you do to someone; it is what you do for someone."

You must keep hope alive within a person. Moreover, you must always strengthen your players belief that life's struggle will produce a more promising future. Your actions will build an intimate and very supportive relationship. A relationship that is based on mutual participation and not on pure authority will result in a renewal that transforms inner critics into inner supporters. A coach always sees the good in you and it is his or her job to bring the good out. A coach accomplishes this feat by first believing in you and helping you believe in yourself, thus surprising yourself in increased accomplishments. It is vital that a coach places you in a position where your talent matches the task so success is almost a given. It is when you put people in positions of your company's needs that you think like a manager and not a coach.

An important key to a coach's success is to create great chemistry, which is the secret to high productivity. Always remember that everyone has great worth. Your job is to bring out the best in good people. You need to give them the dignities they deserve by genuinely believing in them and trusting them with the task. Create an environment that is safe, fun, and exciting. Keep the vision before them often so they know that they are a part of something bigger and more important than themselves. Allow them to learn that by giving more they will get more. They will soon discover that they will be better off because they are part of your team. They will look forward to Monday. Good chemistry will cause ordinary people to accomplish extraordinary tasks.

Another important key is to create loyalty. The solution today is to coach up instead of managing down. How do you find good people? You don't. They find you. When you show leadership by properly developing people, they will be attracted to you. How do you keep good people? You don't pay them! When I make that statement in my seminars, I wish you could be facing the room and see the funny looks I get. The point is you cannot buy loyalty. Money doesn't produce it. What produces loyalty is when a person/coach helps another live a better life by learning a new discipline that improves the overall balance in their lives. They say, "Because of you, I'm a better person both at work and at home." When people feel they are growing, learning, and making a difference, that's when they become dedicated to the vision and will go the extra mile. Their financial reward is built into the success of the company and project.

All great coaches find ways to change up the game plan to get tried and true results. Different competitions, changing up strategies, having employee input ideas from the field, all work to get your team engaged in the company's goals and have some friendly competition to bolster energy for production. A manager without a coaching strategy might simply post the goals of the company for the quarter and give no input as to how to achieve them. This kind of manager is relying on the talents of the sales staff, but not enhancing or improving past performance. Yes, the coaching up manager is going to have to be creative, and business owners should look for that quality in hiring a coach for your team. Coaches, study your competition. There are strategies out there that are proven in the marketplace and that you should follow, just like the skills to make a three-point jumper shot at the buzzer at the end of a game. Perfect practice makes perfect performance. Follow your team on the road to lead them to continue to follow proven principles your company has set. But by all means, have some fun with some friendly competition.

Any company that arranges to have me come in to conduct a one-day workshop knows that I am a big believer in discipline. When you change, everything will change for you. Nothing changes until you do. Once you change, everything around you changes. The secret to failure is a few uncorrected errors of judgment that are repeated every day. On the other hand, the secret to success is a few simple but effective disciplines practiced every day. Again, practice makes perfect. Each new discipline perfected positively affects the rest of the team. It's the coach's duty to set an atmosphere that rewards and encourages the disciplines that results in higher productivity.

During these uncertain and changing times, those that take the name of a "coach" lead with a positive, confident, "can-do" approach to life and business which is so needed with the people I see each week. The feedback I receive from investing hundreds of hours each year with people is that they want a leader with a coaching focus, not a managing agenda. The difference being that leadership is all about people and management is all about things. You coach people and manage things. These people want to believe that we all are a part of a journey, and this is not just a job or a task.

People seem to gravitate to individuals with a "can-do" attitude and not those who have some reason why something can't be done. It is when the pressure is on that the name coach becomes so important. A manager thinks one way and a coach thinks another. The effective coach states, "I asked you to be on this team because I believe in who you are as a person, not just as a player." The good coaches see what is good on the inside and brings it out. A manager seems to see what is on the outside and pushes it in. The greatest part of the coaching up mentality is that you, as a leader, learn new strategies for improving performance. Anybody can demand something from someone, but it is the great that learn how to coach and inspire to bring the best out of others. What a gift to achieve during your lifetime on this earth.

The good life rules, when you are coaching up. ■

Bryan Dodge

Professional speaker, radio personality, and author Bryan Dodge probably holds the record of being the busiest communicator in America. For over 20 years, he has been a popular choice for corporate events, conferences, and conventions. Last year alone he made well over 150 speaking appearances all across the United States and Canada. His inspirational keynotes are on the subjects of personal and professional development, success habits of the wealthy, and leadership principles. The underlying thesis of all of Bryan Dodge's teachings is that "Life is too short not to be happy, and life is too long not to do well." His programs are designed to accelerate your personal and professional growth and produce the favorable results you're looking for in life.

The Good Life Rules: Eight Keys to Being Your Best at Work and at Play *is his latest book, and is published by McGraw-Hill. He is also the author of three professional development audio programs,* How to Build a Better You, How to Build a Complete Sales Person, *and* How to Build a Purpose Guided Life *as well as being the co-author of the book* Becoming the Obvious Choice *which has sold over 200,000 copies. Bryan is also the host of the "Build a Better You" Radio Show on Dallas/ Fort Worth's premier Radio Station, WBAP 820 AM.*

At all of his events, he continually stresses the importance of keeping your professional life and personal life in balance. Bryan practices what he teaches when he says that he goes home to his most important job: being an involved and dedicated husband and father. Bryan married college sweetheart, Margaret. They have three adult children and live near Dallas, Texas.

Contact Bryan at Dodge Development, Inc., 423 W. Wheatland Road, Suite 102, Duncanville, TX 75116, 972-780-7459, 800-473-1698, fax 972-572-9401, bryan@bryandodge.com, or www.bryandodge.com.

Making Jenna Decisions

by David Phelps, D.D.S.

T he Call

What would you do if you got "the call?" You know the call to which I am referring. The call with news of a loved one or close friend who has suffered a life-threatening illness or injury. It might be a parent, a spouse, a brother or sister, maybe even a son or daughter.

I remember that day that as if it was yesterday: August 25, 2004. It was a little before noon. I was working in my dental practice, finishing treatment on a patient, when one of my front office staff placed a yellow Post-It note in front of me and said "Dr. Phelps, you need to take this call NOW!"

I looked down at the note and on it was scribbled "Houston, Jamie Scott."

I knew the name, but I couldn't immediately place Jamie Scott. I quickly jumped up from my patient, still pondering the relevance of this this person's name.

Within seconds, I made the connection as I picked up the phone with my hand visibly shaking. "This is Dr. Phelps."

"Dr. Phelps, this is Jamie Scott at Texas Children's Hospital in Houston." I have good news! We have a liver for Jenna!"

Jenna, my only daughter, age 12 at that time, had been diagnosed just two months earlier with end-stage liver failure, the result of years of intensive chemotherapy for high risk leukemia and anti-seizure medication to treat epilepsy. The drugs were too toxic for her liver causing it to fail, unable to do its job to filter her blood. The problem with liver failure is that there is no way to buy time; there is no dialysis for the liver. A transplant is the only means for survival and Jenna had little time.

Life and Business Transformation

My mind was flooded with thoughts as I raced to the Dallas airport to make the flight to Houston, five hours away by car. Although I was abundantly grateful for this opportunity, I also knew that the battle for Jenna's life had just begun. I was scared and very apprehensive knowing what lie ahead. There would be no guarantees that the transplant would be completely successful. Would it provide days, weeks, months, or some years of extended life? But more than anything, my dominant thought was *"I have got to change my life."*

I had the very uncomfortable realization that my life was passing before my eyes and I wasn't even living in it. What should have been most important in my life had been taken for granted and not appreciated. What you probably realize about me is that I was successful in my business. What you may not know about me is that I was so successful and so busy working in my business that I was absent when Jenna was diagnosed with high-risk acute lymphocytic leukemia at age two. I know a lot of business owners who are successful in business, but absent from their life and family. Have you ever had a similar feeling?

Golden Handcuffs

The term "golden handcuffs" describes the relationship between my life and my business. It means that while I was successful in my business (by society's definition), I was also chained to it; my business controlled me. I was the business. What I had was a good-paying J-O-B. We've all been there, many of us are still there, and we know that there is a better way.

It really is not our fault. Our parents, teachers, and society teach us to get a good education in order to get a good job or career…or ultimately even own our own business!

Yet what is the purpose of a business? Certainly it should be to serve people and make a living, but the real reason to own a business is to create freedom. What good is a business or money if you can't be with your family or loved ones because the business has you strapped? This was my wake-up call. Don't wait for yours—use mine.

Arriving in Houston on that fateful day, I felt completely helpless. All the money, the training, experience and wisdom—everything that I had built my life around, didn't mean a thing as Jenna was wheeled briskly into surgery to save her life.

Making Jenna Decisions

What I needed to do was make better business decisions, but what I really needed to do right now was make better *Jenna decisions*. My family had to come first. I needed to run every business decision through the paradigm of my family and determine what was going to put me in a better position to be with them now and in the future.

As Jenna began her slow recovery from transplant surgery over the next year, I found myself learning to run a business remotely. I was forced to break the chains that had controlled me day after day, week after week, as the technician or "doer" in my business.

What I learned was that the business did not and should not be all about me. As the owner of the business, I did not need to be providing all of the actual work or service product. I realized that I could hire others to do the majority of the technical work and I could choose to perform the client work activity when and for whom I desired.

Delegation, Outsourcing, and Systems

Three dominant system changes formed the pillars for transforming my practice into a true entrepreneurial business. I had to implement systems—both operational and financial. This meant that every task performed by any employee had to be documented in detail with accountability checklists. Additionally, I needed marketing systems to put the business-marketing funnel in place with follow-up on autopilot.

Secondly, I had to learn to delegate and outsource all activities that I had previously performed and that could be accomplished for a cost of $10 to $100 per hour. What is your time worth? If you are involved in tasks or activities that could be completed by others, even 80% as well as you could do yourself, then those tasks should be delegated or outsourced to employees or contractors. This step will free you to do the most important activity that any business owner can do—marketing.

Finally, I had to establish barriers for direct access to me. Previously, I was continually interrupted by vendors, employees, and routine client issues. With good system implementation, delegation, and outsourcing, the need for people to have direct access to me became minimal. This meant that I could be much more productive and accomplish or direct the projects that would elevate my business to new levels of productivity and efficiency, without the need for me to be present at the business more than 10% of the time.

Jenna struggled for an entire year after her transplant surgery, spending weeks and months in the hospital in Houston dealing with complications. With my new ability to run my business remotely, rather than my business running me, I was able to be with Jenna, whether she was sick or well.

My Proudest Moment

I am blessed and grateful that Jenna has now survived seven years of post-transplant life. My proudest moment came in October, 2010, when I was able to escort Jenna at her high school homecoming court as a junior princess. She received a standing ovation and I could not hide my tears of pride and joy.

My wake-up call forced me to seek and implement changes in

my life and business that I would have likely never made without this "reason why." It has allowed me to completely reconfigure the way I live my life and to leverage into multiple other business opportunities without being chained to any one of them.

These are life-changing principles that are not taught in even the most esteemed academic institutions. These are the hidden secrets that are revealed only to those who are ready and open to change; those who are prepared to go against the grain and industry norms of our society and conventional business models. One must be prepared to be different and accept the criticism and negativity that will certainly follow such renegade thinking and action.

Which Lifestyle Will You Choose?

Let me ask you a question…which lifestyle will you choose? Life is what God gives you. Style is what you make of it. Your business is not your life.

Allow me to make three small suggestions. One, put your family first, above and beyond your business. Second, make significant decisions now to control your business. Don't let your business control you. Finally, let me serve as your inspiration and wake up call so that you can have freedom in your business and life, for you and your family. ∎

David Phelps, D.D.S.

David Phelps, D.D.S., owned and operated a private dental practice for over twenty years while simultaneously building a significant investment portfolio in single-family real estate. He is the winner of the prestigious Glazer-Kennedy Insider Circle Professional Practice Marketer of the Year award.

Today, David shows other dentists and professional practice owners how to develop viable practice transition and exit strategies that provide freedom options to fit their lifestyle. He has also created boot camps and done-for-you real estate investment opportunities and strategies to provide passive income and wealth creation. To learn more about David, visit his website at www.DentistFreedom.com, www.DavidPhelpsInternational.com or contact him at 519 E. IH 30, # 246, Rockwall, TX 75087.

Chapter
6

Financial Peace and Happiness

Your Relationship to Money
by Loral Langemeier

S ince money is important in our society, not having enough can be very scary. If money (or the lack of it) is stressing you out, then it's high time you do something about it. Do you want my advice? Eliminate your stress over money by making more of it. (I know what you're thinking—that's not easy!)

Wait a minute! If that is what you're thinking, you need to examine your relationship to money. More often than not, the difference between having money and being broke can be boiled down to the conversation you have with yourself.

I'm going to help you have a new conversation.

Stress about money is usually self-inflicted. To put an end to that stress, the first thing you need to do is become more positive about money. How will that help? It will change the way you manage it. Believe it or not, small changes in your thinking can make a big difference in your bank account!

The truth is you'll have a hard time increasing your income with a negative attitude. Instead of being fearful over money, be optimistic. Visualize yourself having enough to pay your bills and enjoying the finer things in life. What would it feel like to have that certain dollar amount in your bank account? Focus on that image and keep it foremost in your mind.

When you're optimistic about money (and wealth) instead of

being afraid of not having enough, you'll be on the path to over-coming adversity and creating the life you want.

So, let's get started right here, right now.

Assess Your Limiting Beliefs

Money is one of those things everyone has strong opinions about. You may be aware of your opinions, or not, but close analysis is ab-solutely necessary.

When you were young, you may have been told by your parents that money doesn't grow on trees (or something along those lines). If you're holding onto that belief now, your own mindset could be holding you back from attracting money. Money doesn't grow on trees, but there is an abundant amount of it for everyone, including you. However, if you believe that money is scarce, that belief will keep it far away from you.

Money is a part of life. Changing the way you think about it can literally change your life. Take a look at your beliefs. From now on, whether your conversation about money is in your head or spoken out loud, keep it positive. When you catch yourself being negative realize that those thoughts are false beliefs.

Start by analyzing all of the things you believe about money. In fact, write them down. You need to thoroughly explore your thoughts so you can embrace new habits that make a real difference.

For example, do you believe you have to work hard your whole life to get rich? Add that to your list. Also include all of the things your friends, parents, and relatives said about money when you were growing up. For example, did you hear your parents or grandparents say money is the root of all evil? (Don't analyze your thoughts just yet. Simply write down what you believe and what you heard growing up.)

Once you've done that, take on one "belief" at a time. Examine each of your negative thoughts that you've wrapped around mon-ey. Do you really believe those things? Why do you believe them? Why not? What experiences support or disprove those beliefs?

It could take several days to work through your list. That's okay.

At the end you will have a new belief system about money. Chances are the things you thought you believed about money aren't true. For instance, the biblical verse is actually the love of money is the root of all evil. Contrary to Gordon Gekko's *Greed is Good* speech that he gave to the Teldar Paper shareholders in the movie, greed is not good. But money IS good. Not only can it make your life easier, you can do a lot of good through philanthropy once you have more of it.

Let's explore ways to turn your negative conversation into a positive one.

Affirmations

"Everything I touch turns to gold!"

Use affirmations to eliminate any negative thoughts you hold about money. It can take time to change your conversation in your head because it comes from deep within your psyche, but get started replacing your negative thoughts with positive ones immediately.

When you recognize a negative money thought, stop and replace it with a positive one. Write down the positive one and repeat it several times per day. Becoming conscious of your thoughts about money is the first step. Changing them to positive thoughts is the powerful second step.

Good Habits

Embrace your affirmations and new beliefs to create good money habits. These don't have to be major life changes. Small changes can make a big difference. For example, even if you start setting aside as little as $25 each week in a savings account, you're reinforcing positive thoughts with action. This small step can reap large rewards. Pay yourself first. Once you've contributed to your growth fund, then you can start eliminating your bad debt (credit cards, revolving accounts, etc.) by adding a little more money to each payment. Again, it's a small step, but one that can help you feel positive about your money.

Why This Is Important

How you think about money is the single most important factor that determines whether you will ever achieve financial freedom. If you want more money in your life it's essential to develop a positive money mindset. I can't stress that enough!

As long as you hold on to negative and incorrect beliefs about money, you will never create the wealth you desire and deserve.

Money Should be Sought After, Not Avoided

Think about money as a tool. After all, it's more often used to do good things than to do bad things. Think about the wonderful charities that have been able to help people all around the world when they're given large donations. Appreciate all the good that money is used for. It can be used to make positive changes in the world.

In fact, the act of giving money away is another way you can develop a positive money mindset. Wanting to hang onto every cent you have is a sign of a stingy mindset and reinforces the idea that there's not enough of it. Giving reinforces the concept of abundance.

Be Happy For Those Who Have Money

When someone else has money, don't resent their success. If you have feelings of jealousy, that will only hold you back from achieving your own wealth and success. Instead, be happy for them and remember that there is enough wealth for you too, and your turn will come.

By making these changes in how you think about money, you will be on your way to developing a positive money mindset. Once you begin thinking about money in a positive way, you will be on the path to achieving your own wealth.

Attracting Wealth

I know some of you are "hard sells" when it comes to talking about building wealth. I get that. I also get that it's much easier to say it's not realistic. That's a scapegoat. With that kind of "realistic" thinking, you'll never get very far.

The truth is, the U.S. has the largest population of millionaires in the world. Of those, the majority earned their millions through creating wealth of their own, e.g. business owners. About 80% of millionaires are first generation, which means they worked hard and smart for their money. Two-thirds of the millionaires are self-employed, with 75% of them entrepreneurs. That's HUGE!

What's holding you back? To be a part of this group you need to apply actions to your newly found mindset and relationship to money.

Be Willing to Take Risks

Some people never experience the financial fulfillment they crave because they're afraid of failing. Failure isn't something to be feared. Instead of procrastinating and being afraid of failing, plan your actions carefully so you will be prepared no matter what happens.

Take Action

Where your money is concerned, you need to take action. If you've been waiting for wealth to come along and find you, it's time to start taking action to create wealth instead. If you own a business, be prepared to work harder and offer better services. Take positive steps that will help you create wealth.

Invest Your Money Wisely

Make your money work for you. The wealthy don't keep their money in savings accounts. To protect the money you have and ensure it continues to grow, it should be invested in a fund that's well-balanced between safe investments and risks. This is how the wealthy use money to create more wealth.

For many it's their mindset that tells them that it's "just not realistic" to think becoming a millionaire is within their reach. Because of this, they never start something that could be very real. Here's what's real...

Millionaires Have a Plan

You need a plan. It's your road map to wealth. Be specific and learn to adapt and recognize opportunity. Most millionaires are entrepreneurs who stayed the course.

Millionaires Work

If you want to be a millionaire, you're going to have to work. It's true. You've got to get serious, be consistent, and put in the time. The majority of millionaires are business owners and work about 45 hours or more per week.

Millionaires Don't Spend What They Don't Have

Millionaires shop smart. They look for deals. The smart ones live at a comfortable middle class spending plan. Fact: 43% of millionaires have a Sears card. On that same note, most only carry one major credit card and pay it off at the end of each month. If they want something they devise a plan to get it.

Millionaires Make Sure Every Dollar Goes to Support Continued Wealth...Period!

Simply put, you need a cash machine, a business that will sustain a continuous flow of income.

Millionaires Are in a Cycle of Continuous Learning

In fact, most millionaires have a mentor or copied a successful business and/or personal strategy model. You've got to keep up with the times. The phrase "nothing new under the sun" no longer applies in this information age. Keep your mind sharp for new opportunities.

I know the prospect of becoming a millionaire may seem farfetched to you today, but changing your relationship to money is the first step. My personal experience with thousands of clients tells me you can achieve the kind of financial freedom you want.

When you develop the right mindset toward money, take smart

actions, and manage your money wisely, you will become a person who creates wealth and stop being someone who is afraid of not having enough.

So, how's *your* relationship to money? ■

Loral Langemeier

One of today's most visible and innovating money experts, Loral Langemeier, CEO/Founder of Live Out Loud, international speaker, and money expert, continues to expand her horizons, even through the challenging obstacles of today's economy. As one of the only women leading the conversation about money, Loral has spurred thousands of success stories around the world by giving people simple tools to generate cash and build wealth. She is the author of 4 best-sellers, including **The Millionaire Maker** *3 book series and* **Put More Cash In Your Pocket.** *Loral has appeared on CNN, CNBC, The Street, Fox News Channel, Fox Business Channel, The View and The Dr. Phil Show. For additional information visit her website at www.LiveOutLoud.com*

cᴏᵛᴏ

Establishing a Trust Culture:
25 Years of Caring for People

by Dr. Scott Peterson

S treamlining businesses, increasing profitability, and helping others create the lifestyle they desire is a central focus that allows successful people to thrive.

There are three simple secrets that you can begin using today that will bring big smiles and deliver happiness to everyone involved in your business.

I am a dentist, but don't let that scare you away. You see, I have dared to be a "Difference Maker" and I'm not the typical dentist. For the last 25 years I've experienced dentistry in a variety of environments. From the dentist's chair I have been able to utilize learned communication skills, unleash my entrepreneurial spirit, and combine it with targeted, direct response marketing strategies to achieve great results. Now, I want to share some of those same secrets with you to help you do the same.

Building Trust

Wouldn't you agree that the goal for most business professionals is to achieve less stress, better communication and positive results in their businesses while still being able to enjoy their families, hobbies, and passions? Then why do so few people achieve these goals?

The passion that we have in our field of expertise often diminishes as we become complacent with the world that we have created. We tend to start to see our clients as just that, clients who enter and leave our offices and do not mean any more to us than the dollar signs that they have the potential of providing. We trust our clients to walk into our doors, we trust them to pay their accounts, we trust them to be just that, clients. However, do they trust us? Do our clients have confidence in our service and the products that we provide? When they think of our field of business do they think of us? Have we cultivated an environment of trust that allows our clients to not only feel confident in our work, but in us as an individual?

Without trust we are not only minimizing our potential for repeat business, but more importantly, we are really eliminating any chance for client referrals. Friends don't refer friends to people they can't trust.

I remember when the *Reader's Digest* article came out titled "*Can You Trust Your Dentist?*" After reading the article, I was scared to death! I remember thinking that my career was over because "my patients are going to think I'm ripping them off, they aren't going to believe me". I would learn that I wasn't going to change my patient's behavior, I would have to change mine and my team's.

Asking this question was critical in developing a **trust culture** in my practice: "**What <u>MUST</u> I do to instill TRUST in my practice, maintain integrity and still BE me?**"

The answers became a practice builder for me (behaviors my team and I could change):

- In order to instill trust with my patients, we would have to <u>create tremendous value</u> for people.

- <u>Spend the necessary time</u> to truly understand patients' needs and desires; asking open ended questions.

- <u>Show</u> them that I care.

I had always been truthful and honest with my patients, but my perspective had shifted from 'about *me*' to 'about *them*' and

getting answers to questions that focus on GIVING instead of GETTING; "what can I do for you?", "how may I best serve you?", "help me understand what it is that I can do for you."

There are three proven secrets that have driven success in businesses and can do the same for you.

Secret #1: Show You Care and Trust Will Follow

I went to one of my favorite restaurants, just a few miles from my home, to grab a bite to eat and watch the game. Just as I pulled up a bar stool right in front of the big screen, the waitress, speaking in a loud enough voice for those sitting around me to hear, said "*Dr. Scott, one of your patients came in earlier today.*"

A gentleman named Judson was sitting a few stools to my left. Overhearing the waitress, he leaned over toward me and asked, "What kind of doctor are you?" "A dentist," I replied. Then those famous words came out of his mouth, "I hate dentists!" I smiled, as I usually do when people make that comment, and I asked him, "Why do you hate dentists?" He went on to confess that he was a "wimp" and that the last three dentists that he had seen didn't take the time to discuss what he meant when he said he was "*scared to death of dentists*".

Judson went on to relate the most common responses of those dentists: "Oh, you'll be fine." or "Ah, don't worry about it, this will be easy." I interrupted before he could finish his next sentence and asked if any of the dentists had offered him sedation dentistry or at least nitrous oxide gas to help him relax. He replied, "No, they didn't offer me anything and that is what bothers me."

Then (no kidding!) a few stools over from Judson, a girl in her mid 20's—a perfect stranger who obviously had been listening to the conversation, chimed in; "Yeah, the last guy I went to wouldn't stop drilling…and I had tears in my eyes!"

My reason for telling that story is definitely not to criticize other dentists, but to make the point that you HAVE TO CARE. If the other dentists had spent a little more time addressing Judson's and the girl's concerns, the experience may have had a more favorable

146

outcome. Something as simple as asking the patient to talk about what being "scared to death" really means. The key here is to build rapport; ask people what their interests are and what things you might have in common, points of connection.

Showing you care begins with knowing your clients, showing them that you care and they can trust you because of it. The old cliché still hold true, "people don't care how much you know until they know how much you care".

Secret #2: Learn How to Quickly Build Rapport and Your Clients Will Happily Send You More Clients

One of the primary things that I did (and still do today) to SHOW clients that I care, is to truly LISTEN to their needs and desires. The quickest way to have clients feel understood is to ask open-ended questions like: *"What can I do for you?"* or *"How may I best serve you?"* *"Tell me more about that"*, *"What else is important to you?"*

This makes them feel understood. Do EVERY-THING in your power to make people feel comfortable and to fulfill an unfulfilled-need. For example, make sure to address the anxiety or concerns of your clients. Taking a few minutes to find commonalities in interests, family, hobbies, work, children, friends, beliefs and more is a powerful way to connect with people and begin to gain TRUST.

A simple way to remember this process is the word **FORM**:

F = Family and friends—people love to talk about themselves.

O = Occupation—find out what they do for a living.

R = Recreation and hobbies—ask what they do for fun.

M = Mission or message—discover what they believe and are passionate about, what their main interests are.

Once your client understands that you care about them, then they will feel more confident in you as a business professional. They are more willing to let you know how they feel about being in your office and how they feel about you!

Early in my career, I was fortunate to have been introduced to rapport-building concepts and the importance of relationships from experts in communication, marketing, influence and persuasion. To name a few: Dale Carnegie, Tony Robbins, Walter Hailey, Stephen Covey, Avrom King, Omer Reed, Carl Rogers, Peter Drucker, Napolean Hill, Abraham Maslow, Michael Gerber, Tom Peters, Faith Popcorn, Dr. Wayne Dyer, Deepak Chopra, Brian Tracy, Zig Ziglar and so many others. These visionaries, entrepreneurs and forward thinkers have all contributed to who I am today and what is most important in establishing meaningful, lasting and trusting relationships. Who is contributing to you and your career? More importantly, whose career are you contributing to?

Secret #3: Become a Resource for Your Clients

As a networker, and someone who serves the public, I have developed a significant Rolodex. Whenever a new client comes to my office, I greet them in the reception area, and just talk with them for a few moments. One of my strategies for quickly establishing rapport is to learn about a client's business and who (specifically what kind of business) might be a good lead for them beyond simply what they can do for me. While they are filling out the paper work, having x-rays, etc., I go back to my office, look up in my Rolodex the closest person to that business and give them a call. I let them know that I have a client in my office and that they could possibly do business with this person, and to expect a call from them. They always thank me and I leave them with a lasting impression of me as someone who is there to serve them beyond the services that my business has to offer. I am there for them as a person and as a client.

Having the intention of being trustworthy is not enough; intentions only take you so far. It does take time to establish trust. Being consistent and creating a culture of GIVING instead of GETTING means you become an adviser, a consultant or advocate for the client. When you treat people with respect, like a friend, you give them a platform to express their needs and desires. Listen and show them that you care and your business will flourish with life-long, loyal, raving fans that refer everyone they know to you!

You deserve to enjoy not only a successful business, but a HAP-PY life too. Happy clients = a happy business, and a much more satisfying life.

Delivering Happiness to Dentists and Patients

I am passionate about helping others to develop thriving businesses. My intention is to continue providing the person centered business practices to my clients that I have worked so hard to build over the last 25 years. By working hard to develop relationships, creating rapport, and becoming a resource, my clients know that when they need services I am the name to call. More importantly they know when their friends need services, who to, refer them to. Through my experience and training in dentistry, management, communication, and marketing I've learned proven principles that have helped me to deliver happiness. I work in a culture of trust from other professionals as well as my clients. What sort of culture will you choose to live in? ∎

Dr. Scott F. Peterson

Dr. Scott F. Peterson is a "wet fingered" dentist since 1986. Having learned marketing, management and leadership skills from some of the top consultants and coaches in the country, his focus in dentistry has moved to helping dentists and other professionals achieve less stress, better communications and results in their practices while still caring for his loyal patients part-time. He accomplishes this by using online and offline, targeted Direct Response Marketing strategies, concepts and principles learned from not only his own diverse experience and the experience of others within the profession, and successful strategies used in other industries. Dr. Peterson enjoys spending time with his wife and two daughters and his hobbies include golfing, reading, and marshal arts. Scott can be reached at www.DrScottConsulting.com

Chapter

7

Wellness – Mind, Body, Soul

❧

Break Free from Being a Victim and Live Life on Your Terms

by Douglas Corbridge

I remember the dreams, full of fear and helplessness. I would almost drown, but not quite. The next dream I was back in the same place. I found myself not wanting to sleep. I was **afraid** to sleep…

The dreams started when I was about 16 when life changed for me very suddenly. My father became permanently disabled and had to relearn how to do the simplest tasks. I had to work to help support my mother, brother, and sister. I was going to high school, providing support for my family, and being a caregiver for my father. I couldn't do what my friends were doing. I hated my life.

By my mid 20's I had a good job working in construction and making money. I also had an ex-wife and a young son. I didn't like myself very much. That's what bothered me—I didn't like myself. Since I was young, I knew in my own way, that I was different than most of my friends. I knew that I had a fear, always there. I just didn't know why.

Realization

I decided I needed to go to school if I was going to accomplish anything in my life. I got a new job and started college. By my third year of school I was not sleeping. I went to a doctor who, when learning of the dreams, recommended I talk with a psychiatrist. Through various sessions I learned the source of my fear.

I had been repeatedly sexually abused by a neighbor when I was eight years old.

I knew this. I knew what an eight your olds brain can make of it. Now that I was an adult things started to make sense. I was angry and depressed. Who does a thing like that to an eight year old child and why? I couldn't get that thought out of my head. No wonder I didn't like myself. Could it be that somehow, at eight years old, it was my fault? I think I had always been asking myself that question.

Victim

I became an eight year-old victim of sexual abuse twenty-two years later. I fell into the victim's mentality. "Why me? It's not fair! God is not fair. Life is not fair. How could this happen?" I was abusing alcohol at this time. I had an excuse for everything. I felt that my life was predetermined for me when I was eight years old. That's what I told myself. I married an alcoholic because I was a victim just like her. We could wallow in our victimization together. When I drank, the drinking made that realization go away for awhile, but it always came back. I knew what had happened to me when I was eight. The dreams had been replaced with memories and the drinking pushed them aside. Now my life was out of control. The alcohol and self-pity were killing me.

Forgiveness

My drinking and self-loathing were affecting every aspect of my life. I desperately wanted to change, but didn't know how.

One day I was in a bookstore and ended up in the self-help section. I saw a book by a writer who said he lived each day with passion. That's what I wanted! I bought his book. He talked about being a victim of your circumstances, or choosing to not be. After reading the book I bought one of his taped seminars. I would listen to them while doing yard work. That became one of the best things I have ever done in my life. Now I was associating with what I wanted to become, not what I was. But, more importantly, I forgave. I forgave myself for being a victim. While that may sound simple, it's not. Anyone reading this who is a victim of sexual abuse will know what I am talking about. Learning to get over the feeling that you have no control over anything. I stopped drinking and smoking because I chose to. I had control. It starts when you forgive.

Goals

I became fully immersed in personal development: Zig Ziglar, Stephen Covey, Tony Robbins, Brian Tracy, and Jim Rohn to name a few. Why was I listening to and reading what these people had to say? Because they all had something I wanted. An attitude. Specifically, a positive attitude. I was obsessed with how they got it, and how they maintained it. They were teaching goal setting, so I set small ones. Very small. I found as I achieved those small goals my attitude began to change. I felt better about myself and everything around me. Small problems didn't bother me anymore. An amazing thing was happening. I started to believe, really believe, that I could accomplish whatever I wanted to. The fear from being a victim was being replaced by belief. It was a liberating realization that my life didn't have to be about fear and self-loathing. I began setting bigger goals. I wanted to be the first person in my family to get a college degree. That was my big goal. I set out with the belief that I could get my college degree. I just didn't know how I was going to do it.

Action

Nothing gets done without some sort of action to make it happen. I would believe I could do it, set the goal I wanted, but never achieve the goal. I always waited for the letdown to happen. I felt entitled because I was a victim. Now the personal development gurus were telling me I wasn't the victim any longer. I was entitled to nothing. I had to take action to get what I wanted. I enrolled in a private college that held classes at night so I could continue to work full time during the day. I was taking action to achieve my goal of getting my college degree.

Working and going to college full-time can be a daunting task. I knew it would be difficult, but I wasn't prepared for how hard it turned out to be. I almost quit, and then I found an even bigger goal. My desire to achieve was controlling my actions. Something remarkable had happened. I not only had a goal, I had a vision. The vision was to start my own business and succeed as an entrepreneur. I had a renewed enthusiasm. I had a purpose.

Discipline

This is not the discipline handed out when you do something wrong. This is the discipline that you need to achieve your vision. This is the discipline you practice. I had no idea what kind of business I wanted to start, or when, or how. I only knew that my vision was to become an entrepreneur and live life on my terms. At this point in my life I would ask the questions and provide the answers. However, another major event in my life caused me to question everything. My sister died suddenly at 44 years old. During the grieving process I let myself once again become a victim of my circumstances. But this time I moved into forgiveness, set goals, and took action. I had not yet achieved my vision. At times it felt I was never going to. Life kept shooting arrows at me. I had to dodge them to move forward. I did the things to move my vision forward even if I didn't feel like it at times. More importantly, I didn't do some of the things I felt like doing, like drinking, feeling sorry for myself, or blaming myself for not being able to help my sister. For me, that took a lot of discipline.

Circumstance

Webster's dictionary describes circumstance as: "a concomitant condition or situation; one of factors influencing a decision." We are all "victims" of our circumstances. We remain victims when we believe we can't change the circumstances in which we find ourselves. We live our lives as victims. What is equally true is that only we can change our circumstances. As an eight year old, I did not have the ability to change my circumstances. However, as an adult I have that ability. Circumstances are only a condition. To change the circumstance, the condition or situation needs to change. This can be done with a small intervention. Once goals are set and action is taken, circumstances change. Before I could achieve my vision of becoming an entrepreneur, I had to change my life. My job defined who I was for 50 - 60 hours a week, and on someone else's terms. The fear of not having a steady paycheck kept me from taking the action to reach my vision. I could not achieve my vision unless these circumstances changed.

Opportunity

The ability to change circumstances is directly related to opportunity. I believed opportunity fell into only the laps of the rich and lucky, but nothing could be further from the truth. Opportunity is made. Create a vision, set goals, take action, and be disciplined. For me, this was how I found opportunity. Search out opportunity to change your circumstances. Find an opportunity then take action. Even a small action step will create more opportunity. I was so fearful that I could only initially take very small steps. Then I shared my vision, something I suggest you do as well. Share your vision with someone you trust and love, someone who will hold you accountable to your vision. Had I not shared mine I would not be writing these words. That person supported my vision and suggested which direction to take it. So, I set the goal, took action, and applied what I had learned.

Now that frightened eight year-old boy is gone. Today I am living my vision of being a successful entrepreneur. ■

Douglas Corbridge

Douglas earned his Bachelors Degree in Business Management from Rocky Mountain College in Billings, Montana. He graduated from The American Home Inspectors Training Institute in Denver, Colorado. Douglas has received multiple awards and accolades throughout his career.

"I am passionate about helping others through self development, mentoring, and education. My business model allows me to use that passion in a unique way to help my customers who are often under an immense amount of stress and anxiety."

Douglas and his wife, Cynthia live in Billings, Montana. To get more information on Douglas, visit his website at www.PremierInspection.net or email him at premierinspec@gmail.com.

Riding Out the Pain
for the Ultimate Joy

by Andrea Harrington

Seven years ago, I was a wreck. I had lost an unhealthy amount of weight, my marriage was on the brink of collapsing, and I was drowning myself in work. (The problem was I didn't even like the work I was doing.) My husband and I were unsuccessfully trying to start a family, and the whole process had become emotionally, financially, and physically draining. I had let infertility zap the joy from my life.

Now let's fast forward to today: my husband and I are as connected as ever; we have two beautiful children; I am a published author, and I am starting my own company to help others who are held down by the cruel grip of infertility.

I never would have imagined myself where I am today all those years ago. So, how did it happen? Literally one day at a time.

I hit rock bottom one day in the parking garage of my downtown office building. Most of my colleagues were aware of my struggles with infertility and our plans to start our family through international adoption. Every day it seemed, someone at the office asked a highly personal question such as, "Why don't you try this doctor I read about in Las Vegas? I've heard his success rate is really high." "Why would you want to adopt a child? Aren't you afraid they'll have issues?" "What's wrong with you anyway?"

After politely answering the very last question I could handle in one day, I grabbed my purse and made a quick exit to my car. With no idea where I was going, I started the car, threw it into reverse, then realized I couldn't see through my tears and I could barely breathe through my sobs. I shifted the gear back into park and turned the engine off.

There was nothing left to do but cry. The anguish I felt seemed so overpowering that I needed some sort of release. Not wanting to scream for fear that someone would walk through the parking garage and hear me, I started to claw at my skin. Before I knew it, my arms were ripped apart and bleeding. The sight of it scared me and I knew I needed help.

The First Step

My mom is a nurse and I drove straight to her. I called her from outside her office and asked her to meet me at my car. I was embarrassed by what I had done and I didn't know what to do next. She helped me inside the building, cleaned my arms up, and then escorted me into a patient room where a doctor quickly came to visit with me.

He helped me calm down and listened to me as I described the racing thoughts I was having, my inability to catch my breath, and the inner pain I was hiding. I started taking anxiety medication the next morning and I scheduled a visit with a Christian counselor.

Over time I learned to set boundaries with those around me; my coworkers didn't need answers to many of the questions they were asking. I found outlets for my stress and sadness; exercise really does work wonders. When I started to live a physically healthy life, my emotional health improved too. Counseling helped me reconnect with my husband, and we put a plan in place to adopt a child.

Now instead of just talking about it, we knew exactly what we needed to do to set the wheels in motion to start our family. It was still a long, tedious process, but we were making progress, and 23 months later we welcomed our first child, Hope, home. Nearly two years after that our son, Trevor, joined our family.

When I tell people that my husband and I adopted our children from Russia, they are almost always excited to learn more about the process and about our family. Now though, instead of their questions causing me anxiety, it fills me with joy to answer them.

For Such a Time as This

I recently completed Beth Moore's Bible study covering the Book of Esther. The thing that stuck with me more than anything else in that study is that my past will forever be a part of me. I am who I am today because of the experiences I had and the lessons I learned in my yesterdays. So, instead of trying to sweep the pain of those "infertility years" away, I instead embraced them. Granted, it took me years to get to that point, but I can honestly say that I have reached a place of acceptance and true fulfillment in my life, not in spite of, but because of my experience with infertility.

First of all, I have two children who were created to be mine. Yes, they grew in another woman's womb, but they grew in my heart, and we were placed together through divine intervention. These kids are amazing! They make it easy to let go of the pain of infertility. Had I conceived immediately and never considered adoption, they wouldn't be mine. I can hardly stand the thought.

Secondly, I have met so many people who are either dealing with infertility or are in the process of adopting a child, and the connection I have with them is both instant and sincere. It is also confirmation to me that I have discovered my life's calling. I love people. I love connecting with others and providing encouragement to them.

I wrote my book, *Hope Deferred: Keeping Your Joy and Sanity on the Journey to Family*, to document my story. When I first started writing, it was really only for me. As I continued to write, though, and started to tell others about the manuscript, I realized that it needed to be more widely shared. When I was struggling with infertility treatment and starting to fill out the mountains of paperwork required to adopt a child, I read everything I could get my hands on. Most of it, though, was technical in nature or strictly informational. I didn't read anything that I really connected with, and I certainly didn't read anything that made me laugh.

Since publishing the book, I have been able to connect with people in such a meaningful way. I've had women tell me that their feelings have been justified, or couples state that they have been able to use the book as a means to open lines of communication with their families regarding the adoption process. What a blessing to me! And all because I chose to find the positive in a horribly negative situation. I thank God that He led me through the pain to find the joy on the other side.

Today, I am using the book as a door opener to meet others who need a little extra encouragement. I've started a company to give a personal voice to the issues of infertility and adoption. The emotional side of those issues is so often overlooked for scientific breakthroughs or legal requirements, but at the end of the day, we're all just people trying to get through difficult circumstances, and a little laugh in the midst of pain will do anybody a little good.

I said that I got through those years one day at a time. Being an author and a speaker is a dream come true for me: a dream I didn't even know I had! By focusing on my short-term goals and achieving small victories every day, I reached a place where my goals grew and my passion exploded. I cannot sing the praises of adoption loudly enough. I found something that literally changed my life, and I want to share it with anyone who will listen.

But the real message behind this story is that difficult things will happen in all of our lives. We need to recognize when we need help, seek it out, and then return the favor when we're in a position to do so. One of the darkest periods of my life led me to the brightest place of joy and fulfillment, and it can for you, too. ■

Andrea Harrington

Andrea Harrington is the author of Hope Deferred: Keeping Your Joy and Sanity on the Journey to Family. *She is an adoptive mom of two and a passionate adoption advocate. Through her company, Wool Sock Media, Andrea provides a dynamic voice for adoptive families, couples dealing with infertility, and those who parent special needs children. Her mission is to provide hope to those who feel hopeless and to serve as living proof that perseverance pays off. To learn more about Andrea and her work visit www.Hope-Deferred.com or contact her at Wool Sock Media, 1240 Brownford Drive, Fort Worth, TX 76028. She can also be reached at 817.291.9171.*

Chapter
8

Faith

❧

Hope in Everything, Keep the Faith

by Janine Heydrick

T ruly, a Southern Belle am I. Born and raised in beautiful, historical Charleston, SC, by my parents along with three brothers and three sisters. I am the second born. I have an older brother; however, I am the dominant one.

Life was not easy, yet all my needs were met. Every time I complained about not having something, my dad would say, "You have a roof over your head, clothes on your back, and food to eat. You should be thankful."

Raised in a Christian home, our family attended church Sunday mornings and nights. Then on Wednesday nights, we went to church for missions and choir practice. Before bedtime, we had family time reading the Bible, praying, and singing together. I accepted Jesus into my heart at the age of nine years old.

I struggled academically through school. To me, education was not a priority in life. I did just enough to get by. I started working at age 15 in our church day care center making $1.25 per hour. The money I earned helped with things I wanted such as getting my high school graduation ring, invitations, and stuff.

After high school graduation, I got married, and I was blessed to get a government job with the Charleston Naval Shipyard. It was great being out on my own and having my own family. Then in 1973, family tragedy struck. One of my brothers, Matty, was killed in a motorcycle accident. He was only 18 years old. He had been following a young lady home who'd had too much to drink to make sure she got home safely. Yes, I questioned God, asking Him why? Why would He take someone who was taking care of someone else? Why would He take such a good person?

This was a turning point in my life. I was angry with God and I didn't care much about anything anymore. Where was God when my brother needed Him?

Before long, I was divorced and working two jobs to make ends meet. Thank goodness I had my parents who did not give up on me. They were able to take care of my daughter, Linda, while I worked my second job. Then it got to the point where my daughter would cry when I left her with her grandparents—this was the beginning of my recognizing I needed to change. I knew I had to make some personal decisions and set priorities in my life.

After five years of doing what I wanted, I knew if I wanted to make something of my life, things had to change. My lifestyle was not becoming of that of a mother raising a child.

I recommitted my life to the Lord. I knew there was so much more in life for me and my daughter. As a family, we went to Sunday School and church. It was such a blessing to be back in the fold. Instead of me trying to resolve everything, I gave everything to the Lord who is my solid rock. What a difference that made in my life!

In 1982 I was blessed to meet someone who really cared about my daughter and me. I was not looking for a relationship. I was happy the way life was. Again, I gave this decision over to the Lord to handle. Well, my course in life was altered. Bob and I got married in November, and a whirlwind of changes occurred in my life. I enjoyed working at the Charleston Naval Shipyard, however, I wanted to be with my daughter too. Decisions, decisions! I quit my job at the Shipyard. I found a part-time job that involved having my daughter around and began teaching kindergarten. I loved it because I was making a difference in the lives of children every day. Everything was going along great—the Lord is good.

Bob had been in Charleston, South Carolina, for over thirty years and working with the telephone company for twenty-five of them. He was secure in his job, so it was a pretty safe bet I would be staying in Charleston around my family for the rest of my life. Then one day the phone rang. It was my husband's employer offering him a position in New Jersey. After much prayer, we decided to take the offer. Moving to New Jersey, after 30 years of living in Charleston, South Carolina, was a culture shock. Never being away from home, it was quite a challenge to say the least. After finding a place to live, the next thing we did was find a church. Spiritual growth and development were a priority in our lives. We not only went to church, we got involved in the activities of the church serving the Lord.

Sometimes being involved within a church is not easy on a relationship. Our church was doing a building program. If you don't know anything about it, it is work from not only the contractors hired, but the congregation too. My husband spent more hours at the church working than he did with us, his family. Just imagine the strain on the marriage. It was tough. However because of my faith, I truly believed my husband was doing the work in serving the Lord.

Due to the higher cost of living in New Jersey, I had to find a job. I worked a variety of them. One day my girlfriend's daughter needed a ride to go to take a job placement test for a Telecommunications Company and I offered to take her. When I arrived there, I was offered to take the test as well. I said, "What the heck, what can it hurt?", and I took the test. On Monday morning I received a call from the Telecommunications Company offering me a job. Wow, that was exciting. I landed an awesome job which makes me feel like I am set for life. Again, it was God at work in my life. And yes, my girlfriend's daughter got a job as well.

While employed in New Jersey, I worked myself up the ladder and received a couple of promotions. Life was good. Then out of the blue my husband was offered a retirement package. Yikes! This was not part of our plan. I asked God, "What is going on?"

However, it was a wonderful retirement package and we could not say no to it.

Here we go again. My life plans were changed once more. Husband is retired, daughter is graduating high school, New Jersey is relatively expensive to live in. Man, what were we going to do? Again, this was too big for me to handle, so I gave it to the Lord.

Once our daughter had graduated high school, she moved to North Carolina to live with her Dad. We had no ties to New Jersey except for our church. Believe it or not, the Telecommunications Company had a relocation program available that if you wanted to relocate, you just had to tell them where you wanted to move and when you'd like to go. Of course, I chose the southern states. My offer was accepted for relocation to Orlando, Florida. I was so excited! Then the bomb dropped that I had five days to make my decision. Here is the clincher: my boss was on vacation and I had not discussed this opportunity with him. There was no way I was saying okay until I talked with the boss. I was told by Human Resources that if I waited longer than five days to make my decision, the opportunity might not be there waiting for me. Again, because of my faith, I stood firm in my decision because of who I am—if it is part of God's plan, it will happen. To make a long story short, the opportunity to transfer to Orlando, Florida was still available and indeed happened. With all this going on, this is part of God's master plan for my life.

In Florida, life is good. I have an awesome job, and we found a church—one where everyone does not know you and you do not have to do everything. Life is good. However, something was still missing in my life. What could it be? We were not happy at church. We tried several other churches and guess what? We found our church home at the First Baptist Church of Maitland—a smaller church that we could get involved in. Part of our mission here on earth is to work for the Kingdom, share the message of salvation, and make a difference. We did find our small church, became involved, and life is grand.

We all face our trials in life and mine weren't quite over. The next thing I know the Telecommunications Company started laying people off. Unfortunately I was one of them. Again, this was not part of my plan. Believe it or not, I accepted it well. The Lord has been good to me, so I was not giving up now, and I know He has the master plan for my life. I truly remain faithful to Him. I will do what I have to do because I believe when the Lord closes a window, He opens another one. I went down to the unemployment office and filed my paperwork. We were surviving. The day before my last day to be called back to the telecommunications company, I received a call about a job. Praise the Lord, I was rehired. During this tenure, I was given the option to grow or go, which means I had to go to school to get a degree or resign. I chose to go to school taking one class at a time. Within six years, I earned my bachelor's degree in technology management. Getting my bachelor's degree was a major milestone in my life—not having the chance out of high school, and I am the first in my family to get a college degree. Then I continued my education with part of my working team for two more years where we each earned our master's degree in information technology. Again, another milestone, something I never dreamed of! The layoffs continued at the telecommunications company. Being laid off did not happen to me only once, it happened to me several times, yet each time I was called back to work.

During the last time I was laid off, I helped a friend organize an event. I did the registration, nametags, and the administrative work. All of this came very naturally to me. My friend stated, "You should go into business doing this kind of work." "Oh, sure", I stated very sarcastically. When I got home, I started thinking about it. I got on my hands and knees, praying to the Lord, saying, "What do you want me to do? Can I do this—open a business? How? I know nothing about running a business. I am still working with the Telecommunications Company." In the back of my mind, I was thinking about what if and when I would get laid off again. About six years ago, with my faith, hard work, and determination, Project

Management Specialist (Virtual Assistant) came to be—as a part-time business.

After 23 years, I am still working with the Telecommunications Company. Yes, I have my business, Project Management Specialist, too. I work with business owners to manage their tasks so they can focus on what they do best. I do the very best that I can and strive to make a difference in the lives of people I come in contact with each day.

Through my family values (thank you momma and daddy), and all of these life experiences have made me who I am today. Without my faith in God, I would be nothing. My faith is my rock. Anytime I have to make a decision of any kind, I turn to God to speak through me with what He wants me to do. Whatever I do, I want it to be pleasing to my God. And just think, God is not finished with me yet. I look forward to what it is the Lord has in store for my life.

"I can do all things through Christ who gives me strength."
— Philippians 4:13

In saying all of this, I want you to know to keep the faith. If you do not know God as your personal Savior, all you have to do is ask Him into your heart and ask for the forgiveness of your sins, telling God you want Him to come into your heart. If you mean it, your life will be forever changed. Keep the FAITH—Forsaking All, I'll Take Him!

"For God so loved the world that He gave His only begotten Son, that whosoever believeth in Him, should not perish but have ever-lasting life." — John 3:16

Are you going to "Dare to Be a Difference Maker?" What legacy are you leaving behind for your family and friends? What are they going to remember about you?

Do you make a difference in the lives of others? ∎

Janine Heydrick

Janine Heydrick has worked in the corporate world for over twenty years. During the corporate downsizing, Janine, took a leap of faith, established Project Management Specialist, LLC, a virtual assistant business. Her company focuses on helping clients grow their business to the next level allowing the business professional to market their business instead of being bogged down in the day-to-day office operations or project work.

Janine loves learning. She has incorporated personal development into her studies, which encompasses living life to the fullest. Janine is passionate about her commitment to making a difference and helping others. Her solution is to provide "win-win" situations for everyone.

An outgoing person, in her spare time Janine loves spending time with family and friends.

Janine Heydrick's contact information is: Project Management Specialist, LLC, Janine@PMSpecialist.net, 407-551-0578, www.PMSpecialist.net

꧁

Faith and Fire

by P.J. McClure

"W*e have a fire!"*

I struggled to wake from my Nyquil induced sleep. "We what...?"

"We have a fire!" my wife said with enough emotion to bring me around.

I hopped out of bed and stumbled toward some unusual noises in the garage. When I opened the door, the heat from what felt like a 100 holiday ovens set on high hit me in the face and an ominous, orange pulse lit the smoke filled garage.

Slamming the door, I yelled to my wife to grab the kids and call 911. She got our 4 year-old daughter, I grabbed our 6 year-old son, and we ran for the door.

Our bathrobe-clad neighbor was coming across the yard with his cell phone in hand. He had emergency services on the phone and helped us across to his house.

Making sure everyone was safe in his kitchen, I went back outside to survey the situation.

Earlier in the day I had driven 11 hours straight to get back home from a business trip. My son's first-grade class was reciting the Pledge of Allegiance before the school board meeting and I wanted to be there. I missed the pledge, but felt good to be home.

My trip had rewarded me with a two new accounts and a wicked head cold. You know, the kind of cold that can put you down for a couple of days. So, before going to bed I took a dose of Nyquil... *"the nighttime, sniffling, sneezing, coughing, achy head, knock your butt out, so you can rest medicine"* with the plan of sleeping in and feeling better.

Now as I stood in my neighbor's yard at 2:30 am, with soaking wet feet and thanking God my wife is a light sleeper, my head cold was the furthest thing from my mind.

I watched our garage door, cycling up and down uncontrollably, reveal and then conceal the blaze consuming two cars, a riding lawn mower, every tool and piece of recreation equipment we owned.

Within seconds, plumes of flame burst through the roof in numerous places. The fire was already in the attic and apparently burning above our heads when my wife had awakened. Had she slept for a few minutes more, none of us would have woken up.

The fire department arrived in a reasonable amount of time and got to work to see what they could save. By 3:30 am, it was apparent their efforts had turned from save-a-home to training drills.

Six hours, 20 fire fighters, and 31,000 gallons of water later, we had our lives and our pajamas.

I had gone back into our neighbor's house after the fire department arrived and told my wife we would likely lose everything. I glanced over her shoulder to my son and watched him for a moment as he considered what those words meant.

He looked at his sister and said, *"Oh well, it's just stuff and we can always get more of it. All of us are safe and daddy still has a job,"* then turning to his mother said, "Can I go back to sleep now?"

His biggest concern of the entire night was whether we were going to make him go to school in his pajamas.

Gratitude ran deep and more things for which to be grateful arrived in droves. Before the sun had come up and the fire had died, we had people from our community rallying around us.

Clothes showed up for our kids, collections were taken up and delivered, and offers for any kind of help we needed streamed in. During the rest of the morning the kids gave tours of "what used to be" while we dealt with our insurance company and secured a place for us to live.

People wanted to comfort and cheer us up. They showed up with their best *"happy faces"* on, expecting to do their part to pull us through and soon realized *we were already through the worst.* As a family, we were moving forward and making plans for where we wanted to go next. Life had not stopped and neither had we.

Yes, we would need some help from time-to-time, but wasting concern over whether we would be okay or not was unnecessary.

Those who did not know us had distinctly different reactions. In fact, they seemed a little disappointed we were not devastated and kept trying to talk us into feeling bad.

"Why aren't you more upset?"

"It just hasn't sunk in, has it?"

"Oh, you must be in shock."

Shock? Really? When you stand in your neighbor's yard at 3:00 in the morning and watch every material possession you have worked for burn, shock floats away with the smoke. Reality brings its full weight to the party.

When your kids take their grandma by the hand and point to charred and soaked remains of their favorite toy or stuffed animal and say, *"I'm sad it's gone, but I'm really glad I wasn't in there with it,"* you realize they have a strong grip on reality. Shock is not part of the equation.

The thing that amazed most people was how we did not take or require any significant time to recover and get ahead. Even if shock would have entered into the picture, I am not sure the results would have been any different.

"How can you make such bold and confident strides this soon after a disaster?"

"Aren't you worried about making a bad decision?"

The truth is, no. We were not worried about making bad deci-

sions because we were not making any decisions. We were lean-
ing on the promise and instruction in Matthew 6:31-34 where Jesus
says,

> *"Do not be anxious, saying 'What shall we eat?' or 'What shall we*
> *drink?' or 'What shall we wear?'...your heavenly Father knows*
> *that you need them all. But seek first the kingdom of God and his*
> *righteousness, and all these things will be added to you. Therefore*
> *do not be anxious about tomorrow, for tomorrow will be anxious*
> *for itself. Sufficient for the day is its own trouble."*

It seemed that each day certainly had enough trouble for itself.
Our focus was to seek God's will and pray that He would make our
choices obvious. We knew in faith and experience that our needs
would be met.

In that 10-month span preceding the fire, I changed careers,
finished a Bachelor degree, and began a Masters all as a full-time
student with a demanding new career. In the middle of all that, my
39-year old wife had a freak heart attack.

The temptation was to shut down or, at least, checkout mentally.
Many of the willing "advisors" suggested we back off and let the
water settle, but that isn't the call our faith answers to.

Proverbs 24:10 says, *"If you faint in the day of adversity, your strength*
is small."

The rest of the world was not going to tread water and wait for
us regardless of how stressful the events of that year might be. Life
does not wait.

That time of seeming turmoil and one disaster after another
yielded a happier, healthier family, a beautiful new home, a new
business of our own, and a 600% increase in income over the previ-
ous year. All because we turned our faces toward faith and away
from doubt.

You have the same choice. Be your best. ■

PJ McClure

PJ McClure is the bridge between your dream life and your current reality. As CEO of The Mindset Maven, PJ's exclusive methods reach 85 countries through his best-selling book, articles, and speaking appearances. His coaching and consulting clients love his practical and down-to-earth approach to having a successful family, rewarding career, and loving life. You can learn more about PJ and get a free copy of his book, Flip the SWITCH at www.TheMindsetMaven.com.

Faith...
Beyond the Blue Chair

by Karen Diane Sims

T he blue chair wasn't particularly luxurious, attractive, comfortable, or even "just right" like Goldilocks' chair, but it drew me like a magnet. It was most often used for watching TV, daily Bible reading, and prayer. Whatever the reason, it became the only place for me to feel safe and secure. Gripped by fear, worry, and anxiety, I depended on it increasingly each day as I became unable to function in my daily activities and responsibilities. The blue chair helped me cope with life. *How could I trust in a chair more than anything or anyone else? How had I been reduced to such a fearful, anxiety-ridden mess?* Can you hear the cry of my desperate heart? Relying on my mind had failed me completely. I was convinced that worry was a means to protect myself and others. How crazy is that? Am I the only one to ever feel this way? Can anyone else relate to me? I believed I was all alone in my plight. I now know there are far too many who have resigned themselves to a life of defeat and hopelessness. It is to those whom I passionately pour out my story of hope.

At 38 years of age I was diagnosed with clinical depression and prescribed medication. Soon I felt like a new person and was extremely relieved to learn that there was a real reason for the dark, heavy cloud that not only loomed on my horizon, but also over my head. No more treading water with boots of concrete! Some relief, yes, but also guilt still weighed me down since I was "supposed" to be a successful devoted follower of Jesus Christ experiencing peace, joy, and love. Nothing could be further from my experience. Most people were fooled most of the time by my calm appearance, but that took a tremendous amount of energy to maintain. My mind was overpowered and paralyzed by fearful thoughts. I was afraid of not measuring up to the standards that everyone, including God, had for me, fearful of being rejected, and terrified of being exposed as the crazy person I believed I was, or to be "found out", as if I had some deep, dark secrets to hide. No grace for my shame was to be found anywhere. I struggled with oppressive and obsessive thoughts and feelings of dread. *Did I really think I could stop disaster from striking by my worrying?* I worried much more than I prayed. Fear has been defined as an emotion that results from some real or imagined threat to one's well-being and it is associated with fright, terror, anxiety, worry, and uneasiness. That didn't leave much room for the winsome personality that I so desired. Frantic attempts to anticipate other's needs and situations in order to avoid being caught off-guard were life consuming. Life was endured on pins and needles, in anticipation of something terrible happening. It was a waiting game to see when the rug would be abruptly and ruthlessly snatched out from under me, leaving me helpless and hopeless, with no ability to cope. So, I fought for control. But life kept "happening" to me. I believed myself to be a victim with no way out and with no choices. Why couldn't I believe that the same God, in whom I had chosen to put my trust as a twenty year-old college student, wanted to rescue me from this miserable state?

In 2001 my life started to unravel. The more it unraveled, the more it demanded from me to retain control. Unable to face the real reasons why this happened until a year or so later, I convinced myself that the anti-depressant had simply stopped working and a different one would help. Finally, after admitting that I was trying to run my life on my own, in my own strength, under the pretense of godly faith, I was able to see things as they really were.

Four major events brought me to this place of realization. Within a six-month period of time there was tremendous financial pressure, a devastating job demotion, the traumatic death of my children's father, and the medicine was no longer effective. Banking on these things was pure foolishness; they were merely the catalysts used to strip me of all pretenses of composure. I felt abandoned, like the dreaded rug had been pulled out from under me in one devastating tug. Somehow I managed to survive through Christmas. By New Year's Day I couldn't hold it together anymore. Every "thing" that was believed to be under my control was ripped away from tightly clenched fists. How far would I helplessly and hopelessly spiral out of control?

At the end of January, the first episodes of anxiety and panic attacks blind-sided me, rendering me non-functional. Such foreign feelings were absolutely unnerving. I had lost touch with reality. In desperation, an attempt was made to purge the feelings of anxiety and fear by talking to one of my dearest friends, but still no relief. Nothing helped to alleviate these irrational fears. I couldn't pray. I read Bible verses over and over, but to no avail. Nothing penetrated my frozen mind. My mind repelled all promises of hope like water running off a duck's back. More despair. Understanding had vanished. What happened to my love for God's word?

This was when the blue chair became my security. All I wanted to do was curl up in a ball. Somehow doing so made me feel safe. Bedtime triggered anxious thoughts, and then in the morning I didn't want to get up for the same reason. My appetite was gone. Not even chocolate appealed to me. Something was really wrong! Finally, one Friday afternoon at work, in despair and trembling, I somehow managed to blurt out something about anxiety to my best friend. She was frightened and felt at a complete loss as to what to do, so she suggested we talk with my boss, also a long-time friend and a medical doctor. He was calm and compassionate, but felt limited in his help since this kind of thing wasn't his specialty. He called a local psychiatrist. "Great," was my immediate thought. I really *am* crazy!" The psychiatrist recommended and prescribed a drug to help calm me as necessary. Believe me, it was absolutely necessary! The relief was very temporary. "Just think positive thoughts", my mind demanded, but to no avail. Where was my faith that I claimed to have lived my life by for the past twenty years? Faith comes from hearing, and hearing by the Word of Christ. I heard nothing. That weekend was spent battling for sanity, but it wasn't to be. I retreated to the blue chair unable to think clearly about anything. That might not have been a big deal, except that I had always prided myself in my intellect. In fact, my mind was my defensive wall to hide behind.

By the first week of February no choice presented itself but to admit myself to the psychiatric unit of a local hospital. I would be safe there, or so I thought. I almost changed my mind after finding out that one week was the minimum length of stay while locked in the ward. Who would take care of my two teenage children who had just recently lost their dad to cancer in the prime of his life? How were they feeling about all this? I didn't want them to be afraid, but I was unable to comfort or reassure them. How in the world could a decision like this be made with such foggy thinking? But I did it. I signed the papers.

I didn't feel safe there. To the contrary, I felt humiliated and extremely unsafe. I just wanted to hide in my room, sleep, and try to feel safe, but no such luck. My time was very structured and I was treated as a suicidal risk. My personal items were taken away and my room was next to the nurse's station for close observation. Four to five different medications were prescribed in hopes of my regaining some mental stability. Looking at the hospital employees and visitors, my thoughts played over and over, "How can they act so normal, like life is manageable?" I resented one of the aides who was especially upbeat and positive. Part of me wanted everyone else to be miserable, too. Secretly, I wanted to be just like the aide.

We were required to participate in daily group sessions and each of us took turns saying at least one thing positive. Impossible!

But, something completely unexpected began to happen after the first couple of days there. I wanted to keep to myself, but the other patients wanted to talk. So, I listened. Hopelessness permeated the conversations and their burdens compelled me to attempt to encourage them. Seeing past my own feelings of despair and seeing theirs, my heart was led to read to them from the Bible. They clung to every word. I read the entire Psalms and Psalm 23 repeatedly. Simple, but very profound. Would I do this if my faith was completely gone? I didn't know the answer to that troubling question. Then, later in the week during one of our group share times, our group leader asked us to tell something about ourselves. Much to my surprise, my immediate response was, "The only thing I know for sure about myself is that I have faith in God." Did I really say that? Did I really believe that? Wow! I was as astounded as everyone else, but for the first time I knew in my heart that my faith was real. There was a tiny kernel of faith there, when stripped of all the facades and layers of religiosity. I had nearly died believing that true faith had to look like something that was unattainable. It had meant strict adherence to a set of rules, with no allowance for honest feelings with struggles and failures. But, *finally*, I had genuinely acted in faith for the benefit of others. Yay! *"Faith is the confidence that what we hope for will actually happen; it gives us assurance about things we cannot see."* – Hebrews 11:1 NLT

Confidence? Hope? I had more faith in my blue chair than in God to keep me safe. There, I said it out loud, but that honest admission set me on a new path headed in a new direction.

After leaving the hospital I saw three different counselors in addition to taking the medications. One told me to "just do the right things." One wanted to simply tweak my meds, but the other one began the process of attacking my belief system and my dishonest way of relating with God. Two years later, I still didn't "get it" but I persevered in practicing honesty with God. Learning to pray in such a way as to ask God to show me the whole picture in specific experiences, and not just the parts that I selectively saw through a victim's eyes, was liberating. And He has faithfully done that in ways that I can accept, even though they may be excruciatingly painful at times.

Breakthrough came with extreme honesty and accepting God's amazing grace. Yes, I remind myself of truth, but more importantly, I speak truth out loud to God. This is key! Pray out loud instead of just having thoughts about God. A new awareness of not being genuinely connected with God stirred in my soul. I had merely been intellectually engaged in thoughts about Him. Unspoken concerns cycled futilely through my brain, but feelings voiced to Him brought closeness. I'm learning to open myself up to Him. Prayer affirms my faith. I am now able to offer sacrifices of thanksgiving, praise, and choose to actively take Him at His word. This means that I know that God is good, even in the unseen, and especially when it seems like He is nowhere around. Crying out loud to Him even when I don't feel like it, as a willful choice to believe, has brought healing. *Lord, I don't feel very thankful right now, but I choose to thank You and believe You by faith. Help my unbelief.* Sometimes, my cry is simply, "Jesus." And this is not hypocritical.

Identifying what I actually believe is not merely an intellectual exercise, but rather a process of honest communication by faith. As an example, my steps were retraced: why does the blue chair draw me in? *Because I feel safe in it.* What am I thinking about to evoke that feeling? *If I sit there doing nothing, nothing bad will happen to me.* Finally, what do I really believe about my condition that would lead me to think this way? *I honestly do not believe that God is going to take care of me. He is not trustworthy.* This is the progression that takes place whether consciously aware of it or not.

BELIEFS > THOUGHTS > FEELINGS > ACTIONS

I go back to the place my foundational beliefs originate. I can tell myself that I trust God completely, but when my actions reveal otherwise, the conclusion is that I believe something else. I ask God to show me what I really do believe and He can be counted on to do that. I may kick, scream, and wrestle some with God in protest, or try to deny it, but eventually I come to the place of humbly accepting the truth, and the renewal begins. Many times my reaction to uncomfortable circumstances is to just give up—and so I do! I give up the striving for peace; drudgery and duty for delight and joy; the miry clay for soaring with eagles; self for others; rules for relationships; guilt for grace—at least fairly often. *(smile)*

It's been several years since my time in the hospital and I haven't received professional therapy in almost as many years. I'm on only one minimum-dose medication. Is trust in God still a struggle? Of course, just not the huge hurdle that is it used to be. My faith was tested a couple of years ago when a friend of mine was admitted to the same ward in the same hospital, and for very similar reasons. Would I be able to go back there and offer hope? I took the step of faith, in spite of my feelings, got out of my comfort zone, and entered the ward just cringing slightly at the sound of the door locking behind me. I shared my story and listened to hers. I gave her something she could hold onto: "FAITH" simply engraved on a small wooden plaque. More freedom from fear!

The blue chair is gone. I don't even own it anymore. It's been replaced with the throne of my heavenly father, my God, who absolutely loves me…not that I am on His throne, but I sit in His lap on His throne, freely choosing to do so whenever I want to be there… ∎

Karen Diane Sims

Karen Diane Sims and her husband, Calvin, live in East Texas encouraging and coaching others in joy-filled living. Karen has led Bible studies for women and youth for many years. She is currently completing writing her first book, Someone Needs to Hear…A Real Message of Hope from a Real Mess. *Together, she and Calvin have four children and three grandchildren, all the delights of their hearts. Karen is on a life journey of knowing and accepting God's unconditional love and grace. Her passion is to share hope with those who are discouraged and defeated. Connect with her at www.LivetheJoy.org and Karen@LivetheJoy.org*

CPSIA information can be obtained at www.ICGtesting.com
Printed in the USA
LVOW110434111111

254507LV00002B/1/P